# Of Endings and Beginnings

*A Memoir of Discovery
and Transformation*

Robert Speigel

For my big brother Alan
1943-2012

May he rest in peace, and may we meet again,
and again, and yet again.

*"One does not become enlightened by imagining figures of light, but by making the darkness conscious."*
— C.G. Jung

# Table *of* Contents

# Foreword

Anxiety seems to be a Jewish disease, or at least that is how I stereotype it. When I think of the Jewish jokes that fuel the Broadway shows from a century ago up to today, the pioneer days of television sitcoms and today, the standup comedians…Woody Allen, Jerry Seinfeld and Jason Alexander, Larry David, Billy Crystal, Lenny Bruce, Adam Sandler, Lewis Black, Ben Stiller for a few…core to all of this is a world view of how anxious we are as we face our day-to-day existence. We Jews know this and feel it as part and parcel of our DNA. The Romans in the year 70 sent us into exile, and ever since it seems 2,000 years of pain and suffering has followed. We should be anxious, stressed out, obsessive-compulsive, phobic and suffer PTSD. How much persecution can one People take?

Is it a surprise that recent research is showing that anxiety and its related disorders may be passed down the generations via the family's DNA? (Dr. Kerry Kessler and Dr. Brian Dias, "Fearful Memories Passed Down to Mouse Descendants", Scientific American, December 2013.) The implications from the research are that Holocaust survivors passed on to their children their horrific pain via their DNA.

I know there is a problem with the Jewish anxiety stereotype. Dr. Rachel Klein, a psychiatrist at NYU Medical School, says that we do not want to think that anxiety is something we must endure, that it is part of life. (Forward, August 14, 2015, page G11.) And that is the reason why you have to read this book.

*Of Endings and Beginnings: A memoir of Discovery and Transformation*, by Robert B. Speigel, is a ground breaking journey from pain to health, from places of darkness to places of light. Using his life's story…and the story of his family… Speigel in a very personal and intimate way takes us with him as he works and grows toward a better self. The readers of this book will certainly find many, many places in Speigel's stories for their own personal moments of ah-ha.

This is an important book for all of us who want to be healthy, functional, robust people. There is much for us to learn on our journey and Robert Speigel is a good teacher.

The great Nobel Laureate Elie Wiesel, the pre-eminent Holocaust survivor, teacher and story teller, writes in his book "Gates of the Forest", this story:

*A man went to a special forest, to a special spot, made a special fire, said special prayers and God saved the Jewish people. His son went to the special forest, the special spot, made the special fire but forgot the special prayers, yet God saved the people. This went on for generations with each new one forgetting a step. Finally the son of the son of the son of the son of the son does not know the special forest, nor the special spot, nor the special fire nor the special prayers; all he knew was the story…but God still saves the Jewish People.*

*Why? Because God loves good stories.*

Rabbi Samuel K. Joseph, PhD
Eleanor Sinsheimer Distinguished Service Professor
of Jewish Education and Leadership Development
Hebrew Union College-Jewish Institute of Religion,
Cincinnati, Ohio

# Introduction

*beloof:* A mistaken personal belief, usually about oneself, that was created during a time of trauma, resulting in self-limiting behavior. Example: *When I was three, and my brothers made me go on a scary Ferris wheel ride, I formed a beloof that I couldn't trust those closest to me.*

Definition entered into the
*Urban Dictionary*, by Robert Speigel

Several years ago, I was sitting in one of the healing circles of our Personal Transformation Intensive weekend retreats, teaching about trauma and its effects on our lives. As I was speaking, I heard a word come out of my mouth that I had never spoken or heard before. I said the word *beloof*, when I had fully intended to say *erroneous belief*.

I was trying to explain that even before we can talk, we are fully engaged in forming thoughtful concepts about our world and how we should interact with it. Back in the 1990s, research conducted by a Johns Hopkins University psychologist discovered that at 32 weeks of gestation—two months before a baby is considered fully prepared for the world, or "at term," a fetus is behaving almost exactly as a newborn. The research showed that even a premature baby is aware, feels, responds, and adapts to its environment. Another well-known study showed that while being observed by sonogram, a developing fetus flinched and drew back when angry words were shouted at the mother.

In my teaching, I am trying to explain that when babies flinch, they are simultaneously forming non-verbal, conceptual beliefs about their world. Perhaps they decide, "I am not safe." Perhaps they begin to believe, "My mother is not safe; perhaps she will not be able to take care of me."

Based on these non-verbal conceptual beliefs, babies immediately form non-verbal, conceptual decisions about how they should respond to the potentially erroneous beliefs they are forming. Perhaps they decide, "I need to stay in the background to survive." Perhaps, "I need to protect my mother and think of her needs before mine." Perhaps, "My father is mean and dangerous—I need to be quiet." Since these beliefs and decisions occur on a pre-verbal, conceptual level, they reside in the subconscious of our being, and are contained in the cellular experience of those desperate flinches seen in the sonogram.

These erroneous beliefs and decisions (beloofs) created during times of trauma continue to lie deep within our subconscious being and influence, perhaps even control, our daily decisions about how we behave in the world. I use the term *subconscious being* rather than *subconscious mind* purposely, since each cell of the body has recently been identified as being the repository of memory: not the abstract concept of the *mind*, which most of us believe is contained in the brain (read *The Biology of Belief* by Bruce Lipton if you're interested in learning more about this). Hence the notion of *body memory.*

Think of how your body reacts when you are startled by an event. You get a phone call informing you that your father just had a heart attack. Perhaps you burst into tears. Maybe you punch a wall. Perhaps you become cold and numb. These are all body reactions emanating from your cells, not your mind. Your cells produce these reactions from their own memory system based on the beliefs you have formed. They emanate from your deep subconscious being.

But let's get back to my story about sitting in the circle that day, hearing the word beloof come out of my mouth. I turned to my teaching partner and said, "Where the hell did that come from?" Immediately I realized I had created a new and unique word. It was not a mistake or *faux pas*; I had invented a completely new word! Pretty cool. I was tired of using "erroneous belief," and now I had beloof!

When you see the word *beloof* in the context of this book, remember the definition I wrote at the beginning of this introduction: "a mistaken personal belief, usually about oneself, that was created during a time of trauma, resulting in self-limiting behavior." This definition also includes the beloofs we bring with us into this lifetime from past lives— but more about that later.

The concept of the beloof is perhaps the most important concept I wish to share in telling my personal story. Because if I can discover and examine my deeply-held subconscious beloofs, and modify them at the cellular level, I can shed the effects of the historic traumas in my current life and the lives I've lived before, create new beliefs, and make new decisions that move me forward to experience all of my dreams and my destiny. In reading this manuscript, please excuse any overuse of open and closed quotation marks. I tend to use quotations marks around my beloofs. It helps me differentiate my old beloofs from my new beliefs.

This book is written as a memoir of my own journey of discovering and changing my most deeply-held beloofs. So, I write it as an instrument to further my own healing, and to tell my story to my family and friends.

The book is **not** intended to convince anyone of alternative beliefs they "should" adopt. I have come to believe that when I am conscious of my old beloofs, I am free to establish whatever new and self-empowering beliefs I wish.

Therapists use case studies to improve our skill levels. This book illustrates my own case study. I have sparingly mentioned a client or two from my very early days of practice in the context of learning my craft. I do not wish to disrespect the anonymity and privacy of the literally thousands of clients who have come to sit with me over the decades of my therapy practice.

Also, this writing is not intended to be a self-help book. Years ago I asked my wonderful wife and co-therapist, Mary Anne Balch Speigel to just shoot me if I ever went about writing a self-help book. However, if you receive some insight, understanding, peace, or even entertainment from this volume, I will count it as one of the many blessings I've received during this lifetime, and take it along with me throughout time.

# 1
# This Beginning

Sometimes to start at the beginning, we have to start before the beginning; but for now, here is my beginning.

This time around…

So here I am; time to come out. I'm floating peacefully in the womb, although it's getting cramped and a bit too hot. I'm aware that the adults outside are grieving; grieving for their personal loss, and grieving heavily for their tribe. I'm also aware of their terror.

Here in 1949, it is popular for pregnant mothers to have what is called a "twilight sleep" delivery. That's when mothers are given a combination of morphine, scopolamine (a drug made from the poison belladonna), and maybe a little ether, just for good measure. The doctors find it quite convenient. The mothers don't know what is going to happen, but when birthing starts they really like the idea, and the sedation. They can snooze through the delivery in a blissful state of narcolepsy. You've seen pictures of someone nodding off after shooting heroine, haven't you? Those doctors who were tending to my mother must have known that the drugs would go through to the baby didn't they? How could they not?

But I know. My being, my body, and my soul know. I am about to be born nodded off. This is not the way I wanted to come in.

I've been resting here comfortably in the womb for a lifetime. I'm aware that two male beings preceded me. Wisps of their spirits are present. I've already encountered and sensed the anxiety of my mother. I already know she is that way from the last time we were together. There was no denying it then. There is no avoiding it now. Wisps of our last times together are still in us.

The doctors have drugged my mother and have gone out for lunch. She and I are thoroughly sedated, our blood supply intertwined, nodding off, mother and me. Both of us are experiencing the event of my birth in a semiconscious fog and physical sleep.

My muscles do not work. My nervous system screams, "Time to get out!" My cells are unable to respond. My right knee is pushed into my right ear. I feel excruciatingly dull pain in the midst of physical paralysis. There is no room in here for me to move. I'm stuck against hard bone. I need to push against the wall in front of me, but my muscles don't respond. I am squeezed into a ball. My right knee is stuck in my ear, and pain courses through my knee and leg. My mother is in bliss not having to feel anything. She is in a blurry haze of twilight. Her nervous system is screaming, "Get him out! Listen to me!" Her mind doesn't hear, her body is unable to respond. The doctors are off enjoying their lunch.

If not for the drugs, I would be feeling the panic attack going on in my body. I would be shaking and twisting, hitting and pushing. My voice would be screaming out the wail of a banshee. But no movement is forthcoming; no sound is emanating from my vocal cords; no air is filling in my lungs yet, only amniotic fluid. The horror remains contained in my anesthetized body.

My psyche and my spirit experience the panic and have no way to release it. My cells soak it up and hold it. It is recorded, encoded, and memorized in my DNA along with the faulty beliefs I form about myself and my world in that instant of panic. All is added to the database I hold from the other beginnings.

I am reliving this experience, lying here on this mat, near my student guide and student observer, in a darkened guest room on the eighth floor of the Hilton Hotel on the beach in Honolulu, Hawaii.

In this chaotic moment of transformation from water creature to human being, a single beloof about me bubbles up from the depths of my subconscious to my conscious mind: "*I'm a fuck-up.*" What? Other beloofs follow and tumble from the unconscious to the conscious: "I am weak, unable. I am undeserving, alone, abandoned in this frightening battle for life; I am on my own." In my battle to survive, I make desperate decisions; I give up, I disconnect, and I give in. I am resigned to this life of loneliness and struggle.

My student guide has no idea what is going on, where I am, or what to do. She is asleep just as my mother was. She has caught my panic and is frozen just like me. So is the observer student. We are all recreating my birth history. It is a perfect storm in slow motion, this replication of my beginning. I can't get out, and there is no one to help me. It is happening again.

Suddenly, the door of the room bursts open and I hear Diane's voice say with authority, "What's going on in here?" I am aware this didn't happen in my most recent beginning. This is new. I start to relax a bit. I hear the muffled talk, explaining what has been happening. I hear a student whisper to Diane, "I think he might be in the womb." Time has been interrupted, so I simply wait. Diane leans over my paralyzed body that is lying on the mat. She softly whispers is my ear, "Breathe . . . ."

Breathe? Are you insane? Don't you know I'm encased in water? I can't breathe. I receive my oxygen from my mother's blood. This body has never breathed before. This paralyzed and stuck being doesn't even know English, so how can I possibly respond to Diane's instructions? And who is this cognitive being inside me who is having these thoughts and observations in the first place? I haven't been born yet.

"Breathe," Diane says softly again. I take a breath into the body that lies on the mat. Almost imperceptibly, my muscles start to relax, to soften. "Keep breathing," she says. My body is numb and paralyzed, and I am still frozen in panic. My leg is screaming in pain.

But this is not how it went back in 1949. Back then, the doctors returned from lunch, my mother's cervix had finally dilated, and they proceeded to pull my paralyzed body out of her body with their clinical hands and cold metal forceps. I was held by my feet, upside down, to allow the fluid in my lungs to drain out, smacked on the rump until I started breathing on my own, and then plopped on a cold metal tray where they tried to rub the drugs out of my body. Then I was swaddled in a blanket and taken away to the nursery so my mother could finish waking up. How is it possible for it to be different this time?

"Find one place in your body that has some energy," Diane prompts. "Check your fingers and your toes. Find a place in your body that can twitch or at least move a bit," she continues in her soft, reassuring voice. I start to scan my paralyzed six-foot-three-inch, two-hundred-sixty-pound body lying on a mat in a hotel in Hawaii for any shred of feeling, any morsel of movement, any bit of energy. My left index finger moves almost undetectably, but I feel it. I relax a little more. I am able to begin stretching and bending my fingers.

My student guides notice. I feel them start to relax. Diane says, "Let the drugs start to release from your body." "Drugs? What are drugs?" my baby mind says. My adult mind understands the instruction and the numbness begins to fade. Soon my hand moves, and my right knee starts to separate from my right ear. It is stretching out! Blissfully, the pain begins to subside from my leg. I am pushing the drugs from my body and feeling movement again. My feet and legs are filling with energy and beginning to push as they were meant to. I am moving myself out of this prison of numbness and into my life.

There is something up against my feet that I can push against, and hands on my shoulders holding me back. I have to get out. I push with my feet and legs until I am completely off the mat and out of the womb. My voice cries out in exultation. Tears stream down my face. My body is placed on the lap of one of the guides and I am wrapped in blankets. I relax and cry softly. My brain is quiet. My cells understand the difference. I allow new feelings to enter my body even though I don't understand them yet. I feel relaxed and blissful and simply let myself enjoy these new feelings. As I relax, I hear Diane quietly leave the room to check on the others.

As I continue to relax into my new life, a single troubling thought remains from this unbelievable experience. Where, in the midst of the chaos of this beginning, did that totally innocent, inexperienced being acquire the belief that he was a fuck-up?

# 2

# The Brit Milah

I don't understand breath work, and I think it's bullshit. Here I am lying flat on my back at the Wellness Institute in Issaquah Washington, a beautiful retreat and training center, in the hills just outside of Seattle. It's been eight years since Honolulu, when I completed my 6-day Heart Centered Hypnotherapy training.

I closed my private psychotherapy practice in 1995 after winning a National Institutes of Health (NIH) grant to study the hypnosis technology I had patented. I won a $100,000 feasibility award to study whether my technology could help pregnant women stop smoking without using nicotine replacement therapy: Fetal Smoking Syndrome was a hot topic then. My friend David had won a number of NIH grants to study his sonic toothbrush technology (the now famous Sonicare toothbrush) and we would sit in his hot tub after long days of work as he mentored me in NIH grant writing techniques.

I travelled to Honolulu in 1995 because it seemed like a good idea to have an official certification in hypnotherapy if I was going to be an expert in the field. I had studied all the pioneers of hypnotherapy on my own: Pavlov, Milton Ericson, Bandler and Grindler. I could have traveled the 20 miles to Issaquah to take the training, but the government was paying, so why not take the training in Hawaii? The Wellness Institute didn't offer advanced training then, and I was only interested in the one credential anyway.

I won a follow-up $750,000 grant to do a large-scale study and commercialize my hypnosis technology. It was the 1990s in Seattle Washington, and visions of entrepreneurial wealth swirled in my head. We were home to Microsoft, Nordstrom, Costco, Boeing, Amazon, and of course, Sonicare. So why not me?

I formed a corporation based on my research success, and immediately attracted a Microsoft millionaire who started throwing lots of money into the company. I was sure I had arrived and was on my way to being a multi-millionaire myself. My partner saw my technology as a blockbuster product in the image of Microsoft, one that would make us both rich.

However, a small quiet voice, deep inside my psyche, knew my technology would never have the mass market appeal of a Sonicare toothbrush, and that my partner didn't have the business sense to grow the business to whatever it was meant to be. I could see the self-destructive nature of his Ego, but was blind to my own. Deep inside I knew I was fucked (hmmm), but let him have control anyway—a pattern in my life that I would not understand until later, lying on one of those mats, in one of those damn breath work session that I didn't believe in, at the Wellness Institute in Issaquah, WA.

David's Sonicare technology would go on to make him the National Small Business Administration Entrepreneur of the year, and later, a multi-millionaire when Philips bought him out. David achieved financial wealth and fame. I ended up broke and directionless. That's when our paths parted, thank God.

By 1999, the Microsoft millionaire who had bankrolled my research and development company since 1995 gained a controlling stock interest and squeezed me out of my own business. He took over administration of the continuation grant (and the salary it was paying me) and I was on the street without a job, income, or practice. It would take him only three more years to tank the company and lose every dollar he ever put in it. I would spend those three years in deep shame, depressed and bouncing from one opportunity to another. During those years I still fancied myself a business entrepreneur and became involved with a number of unscrupulous sharks. It would take hitting a new bottom to show me that my destiny was of a spiritual nature. I ended up losing the last of my worldly assets and along with them, the final vestiges of the shadows of my Ego. I was financially, emotionally, psychologically, and spiritually bankrupt.

I had unconsciously forgotten about the Wellness Institute for eight years. During that time I went from what I believed to be the highest, Ego-gratifying period of my life to perhaps the lowest point I could experience. It took only five years for my Ego to destroy everything I had built in the way of business and material wealth, and I spent the next three years depressed, economically destroyed, and directionless. The Ego that formed so long ago to cope with the chaos of the womb and the chaos of my family had developed a complete system of beloofs that measured my self-worth and value in material wealth, achievement, and recognition.

That Ego (with the big "E") had become my mechanism of survival. However, at this adult stage of my life, it became the vehicle of my undoing. I had absolutely no conscious thought or warning this would happen. Had I allowed it to come to full consciousness earlier, perhaps I could have done it differently. But up to that time, that's not how my life worked.

In its own way, my Ego had protected me. Had it not, I might have destroyed myself psychically, emotionally, and physically. In retrospect, it seems that at this point in my life, the violent destruction of my Ego was necessary for my rebirth. Although it created chaos for my wife and children, my Ego was not able to destroy the beautiful family around me. It was our Karma to move through this time together and learn our individual lessons it offered. For that I am eternally grateful.

In ancient Hindu lore, Kali is a Goddess enlisted by Shiva at a time when Shiva sees that the human Ego (big "E", not little "e") is out of control and threatening human existence. Shiva asks Kali to slay human Ego and bring humanity back to a place of humility and love for one another. Kali takes her job very seriously, comes to earth, and goes about slaying Ego relentlessly and mercilessly. We often see Kali's image depicted as wielding her sword in the killing fields with a string of severed heads around her neck.

Ultimately, Shiva sees that Kali's own Ego is out of control and sets out to stop her before she destroys all humanity and herself in the process. He knows if he confronts her power with his power, she will fight him to the death. So he chooses to lie down amongst the bodies as she advances through the killing fields. Soon, her feet come to rest upon Shiva and she is immediately grounded, calming herself. Her murderous rage stops in its tracks.

When I finally returned to the Wellness Institute to start my personal healing recovery and my certification training as an Advanced Hypnotherapist, Release Therapist, and Personal Transformation Teacher, our teacher Diane blessed me with my first spiritual name: Ganesh. Ganesh is that familiar figure we've seen in Hindu lore with the head of an elephant on his shoulders. He is known as the "remover of obstacles" and invites abundance and good fortune into our houses. I understood immediately how that name fit me perfectly. After all, I had been quite a "mover and shaker" throughout my life.

Two years later, during my Personal Transformation Intensive Leadership Training (PTI), I was blessed with a second spiritual name, Kali Das, channeled to Diane through her teacher, the Hindu Saint Amma Sri Karunamayi. Kali Das means "one who is in service of Kali." This name represents perhaps the most important aspect of my recovery, managing my Ego (with the big "E"), and nurturing my ego with the little "e". It also initiated the healing of the feminine Goddess within me, my anima. But more on that later.

Because first, I must experience the fire of purification in Breath Work. Ugh.

I've come to believe that most of life is a complete mystery that humankind seeks to explain. I've also come to believe that our search for explanation creates much of our stress and is most unreliable. My tenure as a Principal Investigator for the National Institutes of Health only deepened my belief in the unreliability of science, as did a study I read during graduate school at the University of Michigan in 1972. That study concluded that the primary determining factor regarding the outcome of most research was its funding source. Great!

My life became much simpler when I dedicated myself to observing the mysteries of life rather than trying to explain them in human terms. Most of life defies intellectual understanding but is damn interesting to observe through our subjective senses. So, Breath Work; such an amazing experience that defies explanation, but is amazingly observable.

It is now 2003, and destiny has brought me back to the Wellness Institute. I'm sitting on the floor on an uncomfortable Back Jack chair in a circle with 32 other brave therapist souls. Ostensibly we have gathered to learn Heart-Centered Hypnotherapy, Energetic Psychodrama in Trance, and, yes, Breath Work. What we do not know yet, is that this is a place for healers to experience true healing. It is like no other certification training center I have ever experienced—a place for me to heal so that I might truly be an instrument of healing for others.

We each had a hypnotherapy session that weekend, and did a hypnotherapy session for another student. We learned the basics of the Victim Triangle (read *Breaking Free of the Victim Trap* by Diane Zimberoff), a theory that would become the mainstay of my treatment paradigm. And then, on the very last day, came Breath Work, a great mystery without explanation.

They told me "rock and breathe" to get my breath going in the right way. Breathe in as you rock back, breathe out as you rock forward (DO NOT ATTEMPT THIS AT HOME!). Do not pause in between breaths, and when your body tells you to (excuse me?), drop down on your mat and tantrum: pound your fists, kick your feet, and yell at the top of your lungs (really?). Then breathe in and out without pausing a bit quicker than normal, and do that for the next 90 minutes. (Seriously!)

I decide that I have nothing left to lose, so why not. So I rock, and I breathe, and I tantrum, and I breathe. After some period of time (time ceases to be linear or defined in this state) I start to feel some discomfort in my private area. My cognitive brain is cautiously observing and searching my conscious database for a reason for my discomfort. Perhaps my shorts have ridden up, or perhaps I have to go to the bathroom. I hear a voice say to the group, "Drop down out of your conscious mind and let your body inform you." Let my body inform me? What the hell is that supposed to mean? "Your cells are the repository of your memory. They record everything. Memory begins in the cell and the cells inform your cognitive mind," the voice explains.

NoNoNOOOO! That's completely incorrect! The brain is the repository of memory; they told me so at the University of Michigan Graduate School, and they are never wrong! The brain is this great big hard drive recording everything that happens to us.

But now my private parts are experiencing an intense and sharp pain. I feel afraid, and betrayed, and unsafe. I realize I am very small. I am very, very, small. I feel my senses are dulled, but the pain is real. My adult cognitive brain says, "*What the fuck is going on?*" My mind is playing tricks on me. At first I see the scene from above, outside of my body looking down at the tiny me wrapped in a blanket, held in my father's arms, and a man wearing a skullcap saying strange words and messing with my body.

Some look on with pride. From my vantage point on the ceiling, I see my mother sitting with her sisters looking away. I can see my father is a little faint. Here on the ceiling, I'm not in my human body. Then, as suddenly as before, I am transported back into my body. The wine they gave me feels familiar—sedating, but still the physical pain is sharp, and the sense of betrayal and fear is even sharper. I record a troubling belief in my subconscious mind: I am unsafe; *life* is unsafe. Those closest to you will ultimately betray you. I make decisions in that instant: I must keep my needs secret. I must only trust myself to meet my needs. Stay on alert for betrayal.

My adult cognitive brain kicks in and goes to work; I had no idea an eight-day-old being forms concepts and makes decisions. But my eight-day-old self knows innately that the concepts and decisions he is making, these earliest beloofs, are not formed in language. So they will reside in the deepest recesses of my psyche as unconscious cellular recordings. From that place deep in my psyche, those cellular beloofs will shape every decision I will ever make until I have a way to bring them into conscious thought and work with them from a place of safety and knowing.

But now I can work with these awful conclusions and decisions, these beloofs, from a place of higher consciousness— from my wise adult self. What a gift I am being given. I take my eight-day-old self into my arms and comfort him from my wise adult self. I tell him he is OK: it may hurt, but he is OK; that this is an ancient ritual thought to connect him to his tribe.

He says, "But it hurts and it's not right. Can't they teach me another way?" I have no idea what to say to him. I answer, "No, it is all they know." And then from some other place, I hear a voice say to both of us, "You will recover from this sense of betrayal and learn new ways you can teach others to connect with the divine and celebrate their spirituality." With that, he quietly falls asleep in my arms, as do I.

The scientist in me asks, "Can I use science to prove my experience was 'real'?" No, not exactly. Perhaps it was just a delusion created by the "Stephen Spielberg" part of my brain. The scientist continues, "Can I use science to disprove what I experienced?" Also a clear "No." There is a wealth of anecdotal and personal evidence that I cannot deny; no true scientist would. When I shared the story years later with a psychiatrist I worked with, he said, "A child does not have the capacity to have conscious memory at eight days old. Your story is ridiculous." Odd that all he had to support his belief was name-calling. When I asked him to show me his supportive evidence to the contrary, he laughed and retreated. I knew deep in my being that I had been gifted an amazing and valuable mystery, no matter how you wrap it.

# 3

# The Revolutionary War Ending

I am at another weekend of my two-year Internship training at the Wellness Institute; perhaps the second or third session, I don't remember which. It's Sunday afternoon— breath work time. We have about three months in between each session, just enough time for my beloofs to start percolating again. I try to share with Mary Anne what I experience during the weekends, hoping for her corroboration, but since she is not experiencing the same processes herself she trusts my judgment. I sure wish I did.

I come into each weekend filled with ambivalent anxiety. I've been relying on my ability to think and analyze to assess value, and those skills are not helping me with this. My intuition and feelings tell me this work is the real deal, and that I've hit "pay dirt" in my search for answers to my deepest questions. But this stuff is the biggest stretch I've ever taken.

I am remaining true to my two-year commitment to the Internship Certification before making my final determination. I promised myself to be open-minded throughout, and I intend to keep my promise.

So, as I get into position to rock and breathe, I turn to my "sitter" and quip, "If I go back into womb again, I'm going to kill someone". A "sitter" is the person who holds space for you during the 90 minutes of your breath work. They are also student participants and they will have their turn next. Your sitter keeps you breathing properly, gives you water if you need it, brings tissues when you cry, and generally watches over you. I've never had anyone watch over me for 90 minutes straight. It's weird. The teachers are always there too to help with any intense situations that come up.

Of course, as soon as I make my declaration about going back to the womb, I know exactly where I will likely end up. Only this time I'm about to end up in a place even earlier.

I had heard of "shamans" and believed them to be charlatans and snake oil purveyors. I still believe that no other person can "read" our past lives, and at this time in my experience, did not even believe in past lives—too woo-woo for my scientific self. So as I enter into my breath work my intention is to breathe for the entire 90 minutes and to concentrate on my body sensations to inform me. I am open to letting my body take me to a place of healing, wherever it may occur. I count on my sitter to help me stay out of "shock" (active or inactive disassociation) by providing me an ice pack, or a drink of water to help me stay in my body, and with my experience. When others in my cohort share about their travels back to past lives, I listen politely while judging them to be unstable and possibly in need of psychotropic medication.

As I suspected, after a period of breathing, quieting my overactive brain and "dropping down into my body," I re-enter my womb experience and feel the warm, dreamy, sleep of those same twilight drugs washing over me. This time, with the help of my teachers, I make a conscious decision to keep moving the drugs out of my body, and to wake up.

David shared with us the research studies showing that during breath work, when people "breathed out" the drugs they encountered in the womb, and a microscope slide is held in front of the person's mouth as they exhaled, actual molecules of the drugs released from the person's cells are seen on the slide. Slides taken of the same subject's exhaled breath prior to the breath work showed no such molecules. The scientist in me smiled.

But here back in my twilight birth, the drugs are working perfectly and I'm nodding off to sleep. I have a decision to make. "Wake up, Rob, Wake up!" I yell at myself. My cognitive brain thinks this is silly and my beloofs tell me everyone is laughing at me. But my body is experiencing a calm and fully awake sensation. Hmmm…

"Wake up; you're alive!" I am standing up on my mat shaking my arms, my hands, my legs, and my feet. I feel the drugs shaking out of the tips of my fingers and toes. "Get out of my body!" I yell at the drugs, having learned that the physical act of using my voice to instruct the cells of my body is necessary for them to release. "Get out of my cells! All of it! Get the fuck OUT." When I feel my body is "awake" and free of the drugs, I lie down again and continue breathing. I feel every cell of my body alive and awake. It comes to me that it is no coincidence I turned to drug use in my late teens and 20s as a way to cope. My beloof that I am being silly and people are laughing at me really doesn't matter anymore because I am breathing and feeling completely alive and awake. It's wonderful.

So I am back down on my mat when I notice that my feet are imperceptibly moving on their own. The movement becomes more pronounced and quickens. It is a pleasant and familiar movement. At this point in my life I am a jogger, and jogging brings me joy. So here I lay, simply jogging on my mat, breathing deeply and feeling alive.

Suddenly, the sensation in my feet changes. I am not jogging now; I am running. The joy I was feeling is replaced by anxiety and fear. Now I am running as fast as I can, noticing I am weighed down with heavy clothing and equipment hanging from my body. Now I am terrified and run faster and faster. They are chasing me.

I am winded and exhausted and there are too many of them. I have to hide; I can't let them find me. I pull some brush aside and crouch down in some thick bushes. I have a moment to look down at myself. I am completely dressed in a thick red uniform. Two belts cross at my heart, attached front and back to the thick leather belt strapped on top of my deep red coat. I have a moment to feel my age—a terrified 19-year-old young man. The musket I carry is almost as long as I am tall. I am weighed down with canteens and a pack full of gear. I will die here.

Soon the others catch up. They were sent after me as I ran. As they pull the brush away to expose me crouching in the dirt, I see their red uniforms just like mine. One raises his long musket with a deadly slender bayonet attached to the barrel. As he pierces my upper left chest all the way through, I feel the searing pain burn my chest and exit out my back; the pain in my today body lying on the mat at the Wellness Institute is as real as any pain I have ever felt. The pain in my chest and back is excruciating. I am experiencing the pain in both bodies.

The soldier withdraws his blade and I feel myself beginning to bleed out. I see them watching me die, with disgust on their faces. My life is ebbing away and it feels just like going to sleep with the drugs that were given to my mother and me. It is a peaceful and serene feeling into the sleep of dying. Now, there is not a bit of pain anywhere in my body. I am relaxed and at peace. As I take my final breaths, the disgust I witness on my comrade's faces swaddles me in shame. I am a deserter, a coward, a weak and pathetic excuse for a human being. I am a fuck-up.

These final thoughts are recorded deep into my cells as I die. They represent the beloofs of this ending and attach to me at a deep level. I lie on my mat breathing deeply trying to make sense of this entire episode.

Perhaps there it is; yes—I got my answer. I allow myself to embrace the potentiality that I downloaded the entire experience of this past life from somewhere in the ethos, and that it is the source of my beloofs. The beloof that I am a fuck-up occurred at the end of this poor boy's life, and was supported as well in other incarnations I experienced. I brought that beloof along to that womb I occupied on March 14, 1949, concluding that my inability to birth myself was because I was already a fuck-up. I took it all on myself because I was primed by the death of the young British soldier. What an amazing understanding. I don't have to carry it any further if I don't want to. I am completely cured! It's a miracle! I can leave the Wellness Institute and live happily ever after.

Nope—not that simple. Unknown to me, I still carried the shame of the red coat deserter, and even deeper shame from more recent lives. My breath work was not complete even though I wanted it to be. There was more to be healed and David knew it when he came over to my mat and simply said, "Good work...we're not done yet; keep breathing." Damn, David, give me a break.

So I go back in, and I breathe and I wait. And I wait and I breathe. And suddenly I am no longer in that 19-year-old soldier's dead body. But I am also not in my today body lying on my mat. I am not in a body at all, and yet I am somewhere.

I never bought into the God idea that I was taught as a

young boy growing up in a Jewish home and attending Sunday school at the Synagogue. But being the conforming, compliant, ready to please third son of three sons, I looked and played the part beautifully up until I was 16 years old. I studied Hebrew and Torah, and knew all the services by heart. By age 12, I was the Cantor of the youth congregation of the synagogue, and at my Bar Mitzvah was the first boy to lead the congregation in all three of the morning services. I learned and chanted everyone's Torah portion, even my father's and my grandfather's. They beamed with pride as my mother and grandmother looked on with images of a Cantor in the family swimming in their fantasies. I memorized every last word and chant even though I had little understanding of the words I was chanting.

Even more importantly, but not known to me on a conscious level, I had absolutely no connection to a power greater than myself, to any form of God at all. I was all alone and scared to death. Underneath the skin of that compliant and perfectionistic little 13 year old was a scared rabbit. My separation from God would become clear in other sessions, but for now let's get back to that last breath work session.

So I'm breathing and trying to get my head around the experience of having been killed as a 19-year-old British soldier by my own comrades after deserting from the field of battle, and concluding I am a worthless excuse for a human being. Is this I'm-not-in-a-body experience just another Stephen Spielberg moment, or something real? Have I disassociated again as I learned to do during my birth and the Brit Milah that followed, or was I truly in a state of being without a human body. A fleeting thought passed by: if this is all my overactive imagination at work, why would I not have created a memory of me as Willie Wonka roaming around in his chocolate factory?

And yet here I am; I have died in this past life and left the body of the 19 year old, but have not yet experienced a new body, or a new lifetime. There is no "next womb" in my consciousness. It comes to me from somewhere unknown that I am in between.

In between…what the fuck does that mean? We're always somewhere, aren't we? I mean, what else is there if there is not here, and there is not there? Those are the only two possibilities aren't they? These experiences are messing with the very foundation of my beloof system.

So I decide to let myself be "in between" and just hang out there for a while and see what happens. As I intended, I keep breathing.

Soon, a voice comes.

It sounds like my own voice in my own head, but the words are not mine and they are definitely coming from somewhere else.

"You were following my directions."

"What?"

"You were following my directions, not theirs."

"What are you talking about?"

"They gave you orders to kill or be killed. That is counter to the agreement we made when you decided to go back."

Go back?

What the hell is going on here? I don't know what to believe, but lying here on my mat at the Wellness Institute, real tears are flowing from my eyes and I am sobbing from deep in my belly.

"We agreed that you would return to teach peace. That's why you wanted to go back," the voice said.

Through the tears, I hear my own voice say softly as I lay on the mat, "teach peace, teach peace."

"That's why you ran. That's why you died…teaching peace by refusing to kill. Teaching peace by not participating. You were the bravest of them all. Would a coward and a deserter and a fuck-up die for his principles, die for his cause?"

The tears flow stronger, and the sobbing is uncontrollable. I ask the voice, "How shall I teach peace?"

The voice responds immediately. "You will be able to figure that out when you go back."

"Teach peace, teach peace, teach peace" is all my cohorts hear, not privy to the content of my conversation with my creator. Later they will ask me about my experience. I will have no words for them then—I am overwhelmed . . . with peace.

The Creator. *My* Creator. Not that white-haired old dude with the flowing beard who scared the hell out of me when I was a kid at Sunday school. This is a completely loving, compassionate, present partner for me, nothing like any of the symbols I had grown up with. Not the prayer shawl or head covering we wore at Saturday services. Simply a loving, present voice in my own experience.

"Teach peace; teach peace; teach peace." I've been repeating it to myself with every breath that I breathe from that day to today. I plan to keep repeating it in this life until I draw my last breath.

# 4

# The Forest Girl Beginning

I'm in the third or fourth weekend of my Internship, still in year one. I am beginning to feel a transformation bubbling in my life. I can't explain it yet, but a deeper energetic understanding of my fall from grace is beginning to take place. I'm starting to realize that what happened in my life is a complex set of circumstances that have come together in a perfect storm to teach me what I've come here to learn. If I had tried to explain that to anyone in my family, their eyes would glaze over and they would change the subject. If I mentioned my travels back into the womb or, God forbid, past lives, they would have tried to take me to a mental hospital. That's my family, God love them.

I'm starting to see a few clients again in the basement office of the house we are renting. Our daughters have moved out: one working at Microsoft and one attending community college. They are living together east of Lake Washington with the family dog, Akiva. We sold the family home on Mercer Island after the collapse of my research and development company, and Mary Anne has taken a therapist's job in a medical clinic for uninsured and mostly homeless people. She is being a trooper providing the income and benefits we need as a family. I realize the experiences I am having at Wellness are taking me to a new and deeper level of being a better therapist than ever for my clients. I am surprised so many want to return to do their work with me. My shame about my collapse is still so deep that I don't even let myself believe that I had such a positive effect in so many lives already. But now, with the work that I have been doing, I am releasing the shame and not letting it run my life. I begin to see and feel that it is the positive shift in my own energy field that is attracting them back. I feel myself changing at a cellular level. I feel a peace coming over me I have never felt before. My rational mind would like to identify and quantify the experience, but, alas, the experience itself can neither be identified nor quantified.

At Wellness, we are learning to release shame on a psychological, emotional, physical, and spiritual level. Shame is the beloof that there is something irreparably broken about us. My teacher Yvonne calls shame "damning ourselves to hell." Another term we learn for this deepest level of shame is "narcissistic self-loathing." Both definitions fit for me, and are emerging from my unconscious being into the light of consciousness. My Ego with the big "E" has been covering it my whole life. That beloof says, "As long as I keep achieving, earning, buying, impressing, I can keep hidden the beloof I brought with me into this life that I was a fuck-up." The whole time I was growing up, I had the sense that I was a fraud underneath it all. I am learning that my beloofs are layered; generated in singular traumatic events, but piled onto each other like garbage in a landfill.

The breath work is becoming more familiar, more natural, although still a mystery. Since my experience in the inter-life after my stint as a British soldier, I realize that my conversation with my Creator is the mysterious spiritual connection I have been longing for without satisfaction. I had a rational concept of the "God" that had been taught to me, but had no conscious memory to rely on for the experience of the feeling of a spiritual connection. I didn't know what I didn't know. I am still in awe of my visceral experience in the inter-life, but not yet fully trusting that it was "real." I had not yet visited the moment in time I split from my spiritual self. That will come later in a session of energetic psychodrama during year two of my training.

But in this session of breath work, in my third or fourth weekend at Wellness, I start to drop down out of my conscious mind, dip into the subconscious energy stored in my cells, buckle up and get ready for the ride wherever it might take me.

Just when I think I'm going to have a nice relaxing period of just breathing and perhaps even secretly napping through the session, I start feeling sharp, piercing pains low in my abdomen. Something from lunch, perhaps? I breathe into them and wait for them to inform me. As they become sharper and sharper, I find myself becoming angrier and angrier. I wasn't angry when I started my breath work, so I know it is part of the process, a part of my body memory without conscious content yet.

There is always a punching bag and a length of very hard rubber hose at our feet as we lay on our mats breathing. We are encouraged to "release" our anger by hitting down on the punching bag as we remain in the trance of our breath work. When first presented with that option, I thought it was ridiculous. How trite and predictable and pedestrian.

Early in my mental health career working for a Children's Services Agency in Dayton Ohio, I had been introduced to Gestalt Sensitivity Groups—the work of Fritz Perls. It was the early 1970s and we were all seekers of knowledge and an alternative lifestyle to our parent's 1950s naiveté. In these "sensitivity" groups, we were encouraged to practice expressing our feelings without knowing their source: the most important feature being the catharsis of release. We yelled and we cried and we had temper tantrums and we yelled some more. Afterwards, we would hang out together, and many of us had sex with each other. It was chaotic and raw and scary and hurtful. This was raw expression without healing and without resolution. But it was an introduction to my journey, and put me on a path toward healing. I have to appreciate it for what it was.

It was at that Children's Services Agency where I first met Mary Anne, my ultimate this-life partner. On my (and her) first day at the agency, we sat in the same orientation group listening to our first instructions. We had both graduated from different colleges just a few months earlier. I noticed Mary Anne and thought, "This woman is not like any I have every known." I was attracted to her as a woman, but in a way I had never known before. I was confused and intrigued. We were both involved with other partners then, so we first became colleagues and then friends. We would sit in her office at the agency most mornings having our morning coffee discussing life.

At the time I was engaged to a campus hottie I met during my fraternity days in college, so I was already "taken." My general anxiety level was so high in that relationship (and in life in general) that I took it to be true love and sexual excitement. When she broke off our relationship and I found out she was seeing someone else, I was completely devastated and demolished. The shame I felt having been cheated on was unbearable; the rejection of me as a man was complete. Again, I blamed myself for being an unattractive fuck-up. The beloof lived on and grew.

So here I am, lying on my mat with my sharp pain deep in my abdomen, my anger, my punching bag and hose at my feet, and my beloof about releasing anger on a bag as being trite, predictable, and pedestrian. Fuck! I have the choice to go to sleep like in the womb back at my birth, or I can "release." The pain in my gut is getting worse, and the anger is building like a volcano inside of me.

I hear a familiar voice say, "Would you like to release some of that anger?"

"Fuck you!" my inside voice screams in silence.

"Why don't you come down to the end of your mat and take the hose and hit down," the voice urges.

"Fuck YOU, Diane!" My inside voice screams louder while my body remains motionless and silent. I'm a scientist and a respected therapist. I don't do anger—at least not in public.

But my psyche is going to explode if I don't do something. In desperation, I crawl down to the end of the mat, get on my knees, and start to hit down as hard as I can onto the punching bag. I am hitting and breathing and hitting harder. Soon I lose any self-consciousness about what others around me might think. I am no longer a scientist, or a therapist. I am a human being and I am hurting at the deepest level inside. The voice says, "See what words come to you as you hit down."

What words come to me! What are you suggesting? I always think about what I am going to say before I say it. Words are created in thought, in the brain, inside of me. They don't "come TO me." They come FROM me. Is that not what we are taught? That's what they said in grad school. "Come to me from where?" I ask silently.

But I keep on hitting and I "let the words come to me."

"Get out!"

"Get out of my body!"

"Get out of my body; I don't want you inside of me!" I scream loudly.

The pain in my abdomen is excruciating, coming in waves now. I look down at my naked female form. I am a girl, a naked young girl but covered with hair.

Now my cognitive brain takes over. NononoNOOOOO. I have a male body. No way am I going to have a female body. I don't care if this is a past life or not; we are having none of being in a female body no matter what the circumstances. Spielberg, if this is you at work, you can stop it right now.

"Get out of my body!" I hear myself say in Neanderthal-like speak. I am grunting, and moaning, and yelling in animal sounds. I am pushing this object, this thing, this being out from between my legs. I am livid with anger, and pain, and disgust. No one told me about this. No one explained how this could be. When I first came here, I was dropped in the forest by that woman I was inside, but she knew. She knew what to do. The males who mounted me not long after didn't care that I was just an innocent girl, or that this would happen to me. They grunted and they finished, and we all went away and forgot about it. There was no shame. It was mysterious and felt good after the pain. It was just the way of the forest and the Neanderthal.

No one told me about this part. I am angry, and I hurt, and I'm scared, and I don't know what to do. I am so angry that when this slimy object slithers out of my body and drops to the ground, I leave it where it drops and run away into the forest.

I've had quite enough of this for now. I come out of the breath work on my own.

I've had quite enough.

# 5

# The Forest Girl Ending

I am a strong believer in intentionality. When I studied Neuro Linguistic Programming (NLP) back in the 1970s it made perfect sense. What we believe and how we speak to ourselves sets up what happens in our life. Simple. Just change what you believe and change what you say to yourself and you can change anything. Simple. I would discover later that the founders of NLP forgot about the subconscious, or perhaps they forgot to look into their own subconscious while they were developing their theory. More about that later.

I started putting on weight when I was seven years old. My father was quite round when I was a kid. My oldest brother Alan was 13 and my middle brother Michael was 10. Alan was already getting a bit round too. My father liked to eat lots of food and smoke cigarettes. He would bring home cakes, and cookies, but his favorite was Jujubes candy. You can still get them on Amazon.

It seemed like Dad was always away when I was little. I remember taking him to the airport for one of his many trips working for the Air Force. I would stand on the wide window sill at the airport watching him walk across the tarmac, climb the stairs to the airplane door, and turn and doff his hat while he waved goodbye to us just before disappearing into the plane. Most times he would get a window seat on the airport side of the plane so he could see us and wave until the plane taxied away to take off. The engines on the TWA four-engine propeller-driven plane would sound a deafening roar, and I would watch the triple tail fins disappear down to the end of the runway ready to take off. I would demand to stay until we again saw the plane speeding down the runway and slowly lift off into the sky to disappear into the clouds.

I held the pit in my stomach in silence. I had already learned to hold my tears of sadness and grief inside. I knew what she would say. "Don't cry. He'll be back soon." When I looked into her eyes, I saw no grief or sadness, only anger and resentment. He gets to travel the world while she tends to three active sons.

"My feelings don't matter"—that's the beloof. Hold your feelings inside of you; don't upset her any more than she is already—that's the decision. But that's not enough. The beloof stops working. Everything is escalating at home including the violence from my mother. She is hitting with her hands and the leather horse strap she keeps behind the door on a nail. She convinces my father to join her in the violence when he is at home. He is too weak to violate her rules. Alan is taking the brunt of it—even deflecting the violence onto him when she comes at me. She is holding on for dear life as Dad continues his journeys more frequently.

I can't be with my father, so I begin to connect with him through eating. Whether he is home or not, I can share the love of food with him. I know where he hides the Jujubes candy in the cabinet above the kitchen counter. Eating soothes the missing, dulls the emotions and the senses. Ah, the sweet bliss of food. So at 8 I begin to become round myself. I learn to successfully "eat" all my feelings.

By the time I turn 11 I'm stealing his Pall Mall cigarette butts out of the ashtray on the end table, going out behind the garage, and lighting up. The smoke makes me cough and tastes awful, but with those few puffs, I am with my father; we are connected. By the time I'm 13, I'm buying my own cigarettes (25 cents a pack, no age limit), and by 15 I'm big enough to buy beer with my fake ID at the neighborhood store. I am 6 feet tall and over 220 pounds big.

I make it past my Bar Mitzvah at 13 by conforming and capitulating. Alan is fed up with the family system and is fighting back and speaking up. He moves out for a short time when he's 17, comes home, and shortly after goes off to college. Michael runs under the radar and uses his "illnesses" to avoid the violence. He becomes the focus of my mother's attention until she passes.

By 16, I am still conforming and capitulating on the surface, but a silent rebellion is bubbling inside of me. My beloofs are working to keep me safe in my family, but not in life. I attend summer school every summer in high school so I can graduate a year early. I turn 16 in March of my senior year in high school, get my driver's license, and enroll in a commuter college for the following fall. I am naive and immature in a young adult body. Inside, my mind works frenetically to figure out what I need and how to get it. I've become an excellent actor.

To this point in my life, I've never heard the word "addiction" uttered by anyone in my extended family and no one in my family's social system admitted to having those problems. We are post-holocaust Jews trying to avoid the reality of our people's annihilation. We are surviving by being in shock. Perfectionism is running rampant in our community. Achievement and positive regard is the goal. If addiction or dysfunction is present, it is hidden and secret.

Even though AA has been around since the 1930s, I had no idea it existed. The family and tribal beloofs are passed on to me; people who have problems and need help are "weak." Never ask for help. If you are weak, or disclose your true nature, they will take you to the gas chambers I saw in the pictures at the synagogue when I was just six years old. So we deny the existence of weakness and put on the face of strength and competency. The emerging problems in our family system are never addressed openly, and help is not sought out.

I enroll in a university close by and live at home; or perhaps I should say I sleep at my parents' house at night. My brother Alan is finished with his undergraduate work, and under my parent's, urging enrolls in Medical School at the University of Cincinnati. Michael tags along and enrolls in undergraduate school. I stay close by in Dayton. My father is still gone most of the time, working at Wright Patterson Air Force Base and traveling. Things are quieter at home with two of the sons away, and my mother is not as volatile. The artist in her starts a successful florist business and she operates it out of the house she had my father design and build for her. It's his tradeoff for being gone so much. I help out with the business sometimes on the weekends, but most of the time I am hanging around the fraternity house I've joined, smoking pot, drinking beer, and trying to get laid.

My friends at the frat house have hardly ever known any Jews in their life, so I attract a lot of attention and immediately I am loved by everyone there. I play the guitar, sing, and tell great jokes. The attention is as intoxicating as the cigarettes, booze and pot. My grades are in the toilet as I skip classes and become an expert bridge player. My "fuck-up" is in full bloom and addiction is how I sabotage myself.

But I don't know anything about addiction. It's not in my lexicon or in the lexicon of anyone I know. Certainly a nice Jewish boy from a nice Jewish post-Holocaust middle-class family could never be an addict. Never. My firstborn child would teach me about that beloof once she becomes a teenager.

The journey back to the Forest Girl experience haunted me since the end of that breath work session until my next weekend at Wellness—it seemed incomplete. Earlier, I learned in breath work that one can set an intention to discover details about a past life that seemed confusing. I could call on that Steven Spielberg part of my being to inform me about past life outcomes so that I might be able to learn the teaching from that life, release from any attachments I might still have to the life and the beloofs I might have brought with me, create new and productive beliefs I could use in this lifetime, and make decisions on how to operate in this life based on those new decisions. Pretty cool.

I wanted to learn the teaching of the forest girl, so I went into my next breath work session with the intention of seeking her out and discovering her beloofs about herself at the moment of her death. Yes, I wanted to experience the manner and the circumstances of her death. Try not to go into shock here: just hang in with me through this; it's all good.

Rock and breathe; rock and breathe; set the intention and it will come; Spielberg, don't let me down; I don't care if it's real or a figment of my imagination; there is a teaching for me here; breathe; breathe; breathe; breathe; body relaxed; mind empty, calm and relaxed; calm and relaxed; trance washing over my physical and mental being; transporting; back; back; back; another body; not this body; her body; is it real?; don't even ask; breathe; breathe; breathe; breathe.

I'm in her body again, only later. No time back here, just light of day and dark of night. No minutes, hours, days, months, years. No concept of age. Now I am her.

I've produced more of those beings like the one that came out of my body back then. I've mated with one male. He brings food back to the cave for me and the little ones. He likes mounting me, and I like it when he does. The first time they made me. Not now.

I remember the one I dropped from my body and left in the brush. Secretly, I've thought of her every day. I know deep inside that without me, that little one died. Others have died since, but I know about that now. There is deep sadness about not knowing back then; I was just so angry and afraid.

There is another feeling deep inside that I know the other forest animals do not have inside of them. I'm different from them; more developed. I have no word for this feeling, but it is deep and it is powerful. It is a feeling that can destroy me, or help me to learn. It is the feeling that comes when I know I have done something that is wrong; something that hurts another. It is the birth of the feeling of guilt. It is also the birth of the feeling of deep shame. I conclude that I am bad; wrong; a mistake.

In this breath work, I intentionally move to the moment of this forest girl's death. I know in my cognitive mind that as she dies, she is not a great deal older than the young girl who birthed her first child in the brush and left him to die. She is perhaps only in her twenties, but she has served her life purpose of birthing offspring and is ready to die. I am back in her body as she takes her final breaths as the forest girl. She has no fear about death, no beloofs about moving from this realm to another. It is just what is.

And as she takes her last breath in this lifetime, I check into her body about the shame of leaving the young one in the brush to die. It is present, and it is deep and severe. She carries it beyond her final breath, and bequeaths it to me.

# 6

# Coming to Peace with My Brother

As an adult, I don't share much with my family about my career as a therapist, and even less about my personal experiences doing my own work. I gave up trying years ago when everyone scoffed at my attempts to intervene with my middle brother's burgeoning drug addiction. Middle-class Jewish families simply do not have drug addicts in their fold, especially if they've achieved the title of Doctor after their name.

My middle brother Michael married his college sweetheart just after they completed undergraduate school when he was 22 years old. My parents paid his way through dental school, and after he graduated they set him up with a fancy office. Michael always corrected us that he was a DMD, not a DDS and liked us to address our mail to him as Dr. Michael Speigel, DMD. He had become my parents' "son the doctor" and brought them the recognition they sought. He was "one up" on Alan who dropped out of Medical School during his second year when he became disillusioned with the dogma of medicine. He transferred to Case Western Reserve University in Cleveland and became a chemical engineer. That left Michael as the only "Doctor" they raised. I was their son the "psychologist." Oops...

The entire family propped Michael up throughout most of his life. As a child he had an undiagnosed vitamin deficiency that caused him to have an enlarged liver. No one knew what to do until one astute MD tested him and found he was dangerously low in vitamin C levels. The condition was quickly cured with vitamin therapy and increasing fruit in his diet, but his growth was somewhat stunted, and he had a difficult time keeping his weight up.

But the more serious consequences of Michael's "illness" were to our family system and his psyche. The beloof that he was "sickly" and "in need of special care and treatment" was firmly in place by the time he was six and I was three. Therapists call this the "wooden leg" syndrome. My brother came to believe he was entitled to special treatment, and the family members who were expected to provide the special treatment became resentful and jealous. The 12-step addiction programs I would participate in later in life call this process "enabling."

Even though I was the youngest, I was given clear directions to take care of Michael and help him in any way I could. In one of my many hypnotherapy sessions at Wellness, I went back to a time when I was only about six years old and doing chores with my oldest brother Alan, clearing the table after dinner and washing the dishes. In the hypnosis, I made eye contact with Michael who was sitting on a stool across the room watching. He would have been about nine.

Now, hypnotherapy slows everything down, exposing the nuances of a happening that we never picked up in the first place, or simply forgot, but were recorded in our subconscious in detail. I liken the experience to watching a replay of a base-ball pitcher on TV throwing a pitch in super slow motion. You can actually see the stitches of the ball rotating in whatever direction the pitcher directed the ball to fly. It takes four to five seconds for the pitch to reach the catcher's glove in super slow motion, when in reality the pitch smacks into his glove less than one half-second after the pitcher throws the ball.

So, during this half-second in time, when I turn and look at my brother sitting on his stool across the room as I take dishes to the sink, I unconsciously record the micro-emotions flashing across his face: his lip curls into a sneer of dominance and his eyes flash "gotcha!" In the actual moment the incident occurred, my true emotions never entered my consciousness—under direction of my mother's edict and my established care-taking beloof. But in the hypnosis, the clear image and the feelings attached emerged from my subconscious memory as if they had just occurred. In that moment, I am back in the kitchen, six years old, experiencing my feelings.

"Can't you see what he's doing!?" I silently scream at my mom.

"He's faking it! He knows exactly what he's doing and you can't see it."

"Listen to me!" I call out silently.

But she is busy, oblivious to the obvious.

And Dad's at work, as usual.

When I look at my mother in the hypnosis, she's in emotional shock, just as she is when he is 18 and graduates high school, and again when he is 22 and graduates from college and marries his college sweetheart; and again at 25 when she and my father makes sure he graduates from dental school by lobbying the faculty and finishing his work for him.

I see it again when they go on to rent him his fully outfitted office and spend hours decorating it for him; he is still sitting on the stool on the other side of the room, micro-sneer on his lips, entitled. With my parents' help, he and his wife buy a house and they have two sons. And still he sits on the stool. I see him smoking pot daily and using the nitrous oxide inhaler in his office when I go to visit. I'm smoking pot myself, and I try out his nitrous setup under his direction. But something is different—I sense something is terribly wrong. But still I am silent.

Michael's wife finally gets fed up and divorces him before the children are 10 years old. He will blame her for the divorce the rest of his life, and enlist my mother in the never-ending blame game. My father will remain silent and travel. My mother will take a pair of scissors and physically cut Michael's wife's image out of all the wedding pictures she has. She will never forgive her for divorcing him.

Michael will go on to abuse his DEA privileges as a dentist—lying on his dental chair and breathing in the intoxicating vapors of his nitrous oxide machine at the end of each day. Finally he will lose his practice writing opioid prescriptions for himself and his willing patients. The DEA will have had enough. My entire family will continue to prop up his wooden leg, making excuses for his behavior. After all, he was a sick kid. After all, his wife left him. After all...

My family would blame me for not taking better care of him. They would hear nothing about the illness I knew he was suffering from. They would never intervene and get him the help he needed. They would discount my professional opinions as non-medical: after all, only medical doctors know what is really going on with people. In their eyes, I was still their "baby."

I would eventually give up trying to teach my family about addiction, especially how prone doctors and dentists are to becoming addicted to the very drugs they prescribe to their patients. My family really never came to know my world, my work, my struggles, and my own recovery. They would never ask. I would go on to become a seasoned mental health professional, husband and father. I would go to Al-Anon years later when my own child struggled with addiction. They would never know. I would develop a new and healthy family, larger and more vibrant than I could ever have imagined. But they would never know. I would come to forgive them all and love them in a way I never had imagined—just as they were and are. I would learn to love them unconditionally, and in the process, learn to love myself similarly.

Michael would ultimately lose his DEA license, his career, his livelihood, his family, and his health. He would end up with Multiple Sclerosis and dementia, sitting in a wheelchair, living in an assisted living facility. I would end up never having another conversation with the big brother I loved so much when we were young. I still love him deeply in my heart. It is the only place he allows.

# 7

# The Civil War Ending

B ack on my mat, at the beginning of the second year of my Internship at Wellness. I'm actually starting to enjoy my once per quarter, five-day weekends there. My cohort has bonded into a living, breathing organism not to be denied. We are becoming a family. We have all the dysfunction of a "normal" family—jealousy, competition, secrecy, aggression, passivity—but something else I have only experienced in fleeting moments of my previous life: a commitment to each other to work through our problems using the amazing tools and experiences of our proven effective processes.

The processes we use at Wellness are all tried and true, but also over time have evolved into a new and profound mechanism of first recovery, and then transformation. We are truly like caterpillars transforming into unique and beautiful butterflies. It is painful, exciting, frightening, and difficult. Some leave, not able to handle the intensity, and although the urge is with me always to steal away in the middle of the night, I know I must complete this journey. My higher self won't let me run.

This time on my mat, I have another intention. I've only encountered past memories from this life or other lives when I have been victimized—murdered, lynched, raped, cut. But I muse that I must have gathered some negative karma points along the way; perhaps just a few, anyway. My intention for this breath work is to encounter a time in my karmic development when I was the persecutor, the perpetrator, the tyrant.

So I rock and I breathe and I rock and I breathe and I drop and I tantrum. And I breathe, and breathe and breathe, waiting to travel.

And I don't.

I accept that my intention is too specific—too directed. Breath work is intended to take you where you need to go, not where you want to go. I remember the admonition of my teachers: "If all you do is breathe for 90 minutes, it is all good."

So I breathe without intention, waiting for the blessing of the end of the session. But not yet.

A feeling starts to arise in my arms. It is excitement. I am informed that these are not my arms, but the arms of another. I am in a different body. The smoke is dense around me. Yelling, chaos, death. Unbelievable death. I am in a killing field of war.

In my hands is my rifle, tipped with a long slender blade. I am running screaming through the field. This time I am running toward, not running away. As I run, I send the blade through a body in front of me, withdrawing the blade quickly so it is available to me for the next. I see no faces on the bodies I pierce. If I perceive a single face on a single body, I will feel the emotions of my act. That is unacceptable. These are not human beings; they are the enemy and must be defeated and destroyed. They mean to steal my God-given rights away from me. The right to own my property, my land, my slaves. My right to control my women and my animals. My right to do whatever I damn well please no matter what the effect on others. Damn these weak, bleeding heart Northerners. Damn them all to hell! I want all of them to die, and then to die myself, protecting my rights and beliefs. Come and get me if you can. I'm going to take as many of you to hell with me as possible.

My cognitive brain interrupts for a moment. My God, I actually understand this man, this soldier willing to die for his beliefs. Could it be that this present day, bleeding heart, liberal thinking, democrat Social Worker body of mine lying on this mat at Wellness, deeply understands his feelings and beliefs and his right to have and express them? I am experiencing his experience on a visceral level. I am experiencing real empathy for him while my cognitive brain detests everything he stands for. Shit!

I decide to go to the end of this life I am experiencing. I wish to consciously understand the meaning of his life and the beloofs I might have brought into this life before I release this distant remnant wisp of his spirit still attached to my being and my soul.

Now I am back in his body. I am a killing machine, experiencing joy and release in the process of taking each Northerner's life, one by one. To my dismay, I survive the battle of that day, and in fact the war ends shortly thereafter. I survive the war and go on to live a long life on my southern cotton farm.

As I age in the lifetime of this aging confederate military veteran, I begin to hear the wisp of the voice of the young British redcoat soldier unconsciously whispering to me. I have no conscious memory of that lifetime—that memory will surface a few lifetimes from now lying on a mat in Issaquah Washington. But the distant voice is within my unconscious being all the same. "Teach Peace, Teach Peace, Teach Peace."

In the latter part of this lifetime as a Confederate soldier, faces begin to appear on the bodies of the human beings I killed. Deep in my soul, I am overwhelmed with shame and grief. I try to make up for the carnage I had wrecked during the war. I take up causes of peace, but the killing is too over-whelming. They say a piece of one's soul dies with every life we take away. I turn to alcohol to drown the memories and the pain, but it only buries it deeper. I am going through the motions of life, unable to recover from the wounds that lie deep in my subconscious mind. I will die quite old and quite silently. I will not utter a word of my experience or my feelings even to my wife or children. I will carry my shame and my grief to the grave, and bequeath both to those who follow.

In the conclusion of my breath work, I released this spirit from my body, my cells, my atoms, and my being. In the process, we released him of his shame and his grief so he could fully move into the light of the creator's forgiveness and love. As we did, I felt the presence of my own creator's forgiveness and love. I smelled the pungent smell of the burning white sage above me as my cohorts helped move his spirit along. I was at peace, lying and breathing on my mat at Wellness. The download is complete.

After the session, I recalled that I had visited the battlefield at Gettysburg traveling with a friend and his family on vacation one summer when I was about 15 years old. On that visit, I learned that from July 1-3, 1863, over 51,000 Union and Confederate soldiers would become casualties—killed, wounded, or missing—for this country's Civil War. I remembered that day standing on the grassy field, feeling a cold shiver run through my entire body. I felt the souls who died there without knowing it consciously. I just remember feeling "weird." Was this the first experience of this past life attachment emerging from my unconscious being? Was my experience on the mat at Wellness triggered by my childhood experience of visiting Gettysburg? Does it matter?

This experience one Sunday afternoon on my mat at Wellness could be judged to be "real," or another figment of my Stephen Spielberg brain. Was I releasing a past life attachment, or simply releasing a beloof I had developed along the way? I don't really care or wish to engage in debate about one of the most important experiences of my life. To judge it would negate the deep importance of its teaching, and move me off my path of recovery. In addition, it would lead me to perhaps the most important past life experience I would encounter. The life just prior to entering this one.

# 8
# A Child of the Holocaust

I was born March 14, 1949 at 1:30 PM at Saint Elizabeth's Hospital in Dayton, Ohio. My father was 36 at the time and my mother was 34. I was their third son and supposed to be a girl for my mother. There wasn't much I could do about that, although I did try to be the best damn daughter for my mother that an active young boy could be. My oldest brother Alan had been born in February, 1943 and middle brother Michael in June, 1946. My father's father died suddenly, six months into my mother's pregnancy with me, just before he was to visit us. These dates mean a lot to me when I look at them in the context of our history.

Here are more important dates I add to the mix: Adolph Hitler came to power in Germany in 1933. He began a systematized program of persecuting and ultimately committing genocide on the Jewish population of Europe along with other Non-Aryan minorities. He ran riot for more than eight years, building concentration camps to exterminate everyone who threatened him, stealing as much property as he could, and terrorizing everyone and anyone he came in contact with including his own people. Every German had to join the Reich or be shot in the head where they stood.

The United States joined the war on December 11, 1941. On December 7, 1941, Pearl Harbor was bombed by the Japanese killing over 2,500 mostly American service people and injuring 1,000 more. That is what brought the U.S. into World War Two, not what was going on in Europe. The U.S.

Government turned a blind eye to the plight of European Jews for eight long years. My parents married on February 23, 1941, just months before the U.S. entered the war. They were introduced to each other by a mutual friend. My father Jack (Jacob) was 28 when they married and my mother Sylvia was 26. Jack worked designing guns at the Springfield Massachusetts Firearms Armory when the war broke out. He dropped out of MIT in 1940 to help support his immigrant parents who were not doing well. He dreamed of becoming an architect and designing homes for people. The war and the security of working for the United States Air Force as a civilian armaments designer brought him to Wright Patterson Air Force Base in Dayton, Ohio shortly after they married. My father helped design most of the gunnery for the B-24 bomber that was used late in the war. Our family lived a drivable distance from my mother's family in Louisville Kentucky.

Here is what was happening in Europe in 1941 during Jack and Sylvia's first year of marriage:

January 21–26: Anti-Jewish riots in Romania, hundreds of Jews butchered.

February 1: German authorities begin rounding up Polish Jews for transfer to Warsaw Ghetto. Ten thousand Jews died by starvation in the ghetto between January and June 1941.

March: Adolf Eichmann appointed head of the department for Jewish affairs of the Reich Security Main Office, Section IV B 4.

April 6: Germany attacks Yugoslavia and Greece: occupation follows.

April 21: Natzweiler-Struthof concentration camp opens in France.

June 22: Germany invades the Soviet Union.

July 31: Heydrich appointed by Göring to implement the "Final Solution."

July–August: Thousands of Russian Jews are murdered by the Einzatzgruppen (extermination squads) in the occupied territories. Here are some examples:

5,200 Jews murdered in Byalistok.

2,000 Jews murdered in Minsk.

5,000 Jews murdered in Vilna.

5,000 Jews murdered in Brest-Litovsk.

5,000 Jews murdered in Tarnopol.

3,500 Jews murdered in Zloczow.

11,000 Jews murdered in Pinsk.

14,000 Jews murdered in Kamenets Podolsk.

12,287 Jews murdered in Kishinev.

Alan came along in February, 1943. This was happening then:

January: German 6th Army surrenders at Stalingrad.

March: Liquidation of Krakow ghetto.

April: Previously POW camp Bergen-Belsen is under SS control.

April 19: Warsaw Ghetto revolt begins as Germans attempt to liquidate 70,000 inhabitants; Jewish underground fights Nazis until early June.

June: Himmler orders the liquidation of all ghettos in Poland and the Soviet Union.

Summer: Armed resistance by Jews in Bedzin, Bialystok, Czestochowa, Lvov, and Tarnow ghettos.

Fall: Liquidation of large ghettos in Minsk, Vilna, and Riga.

October 14: Armed revolt in Sobibor extermination
camp.
October-November: Rescue of the Danish Jewry.

In 1945, the year that my mother Sylvia was pregnant with
my brother Michael:

January 17: Evacuation of Auschwitz; beginning of
Death March.
January 25: Beginning of death march for inmates of
Stutthof.
April 6-10: Death march of inmates of Buchenwald.
April 8: Liberation of Buchenwald.
April 15: Liberation of Bergen-Belsen.
April 22: Liberation of Sachsenhausen.
April 23: Liberation of Flossenburg.
April 29: Liberation of Dachau.
April 30: Hitler commits suicide, liberation of
Ravensbruck.
May 7: Liberation of Mauthausen.
May 8: V-E Day: Germany surrenders; end of
Third Reich.
August 6: Bombing of Hiroshima.
August 9: Bombing of Nagasaki.
August 15: V-J Day: Victory over Japan proclaimed.
September 2: Japan surrenders: end of World War II.

My father's younger brother Morris was in the United
Stated Infantry sent in to liberate Dachau of its remaining
prisoners after the death marches of 1945. He voluntarily
stayed for the next four years helping to expatriate the homeless Jewish refugees who had lost everything, including the

lives of their families. He
could very well have been
one of the soldiers in this
photo taken when the U.S.
military came into the
death camps. Sometime in
1949 he came home from
Germany to live with my
family in Dayton, Ohio.

I was born in March of that year.

I remember Uncle Morris sitting in darkness in our living
room for hours on end, smoking Camel cigarettes and stub-
bing out the butts into a full ashtray. I looked into his darkened eyes in the darkened room from the doorway. They
looked elsewhere, into distant memories I would come to understand later. I shied away from approaching him, sensing
his deep need for privacy. The darkness in his eyes frightened
me. He was joyless and I followed his lead. No one in the family ever spoke about what had happened. Words of emotion
were never uttered. Later, under hypnosis, I would re-experience the pall over our entire house of my first few years on
the planet. I would encounter the thousands of horrified souls
he brought with him into our home. They occupied every corner of our house and every cell of my being. They were not to
be denied.

As I became more conscious and informed, I would see
the tattooed numbers on the inside arms of the people who
would visit our home and our synagogue. They spoke with
strange accents and dressed in different ways. I did not understand why they were here. Most had a blank stare of shock
in their eyes and spoke quietly if at all. While I did not un-

derstand the source, I recorded their shock and their horror and their grief in my cells. I entered into the shock with them to survive. Their blank stare became mine. Their horror became mine. Their grief became mine. I had no conscious knowledge of what was happening to me.

Nor did I possess any knowledge of the even more distant ancestral trauma my family carried. My father, Jacob, was born to Russian immigrants who fled the pogroms of Russia early in the 1900s. The story goes that my father's father first came to America by boat from the Ukraine, to set up a home in the land with gold flowing in the streets and then send for his bride. While he found that gold did not flow in the streets, at least his people were not being raped and murdered by the Russian soldiers before they burned their villages. He was happy to be in a safe land. He died before I heard his personal story of his family's time in Russia.

The story continues that after landing at Ellis Island in New York, he boarded a boat for San Francisco to open a barber shop. The boat sailed around South America through the Strait of Magellan and on up to California. He opened his shop and began making plans to bring his bride over. It was 1906, and other events would interrupt his plans.

When my father would recount the story his father told him, he said, "Dad told me he walked out of his shop when the earthquake began and watched the street open up in front

of him. The entire city was on fire. He walked back into his shop, gathered up a few of his belongings, walked down to the wharf and boarded the first boat he could to New York." I don't know if the story is completely accurate, but the pictures of the carnage of the 1906 San Francisco earthquake make the story believable. It must have triggered my grandfather's memories of the burning villages he left behind in Russia.

The story continues that after sailing back around South America and returning to the East Coast, my grandfather decided to settle in Boston, Massachusetts. He must have loved being close to the water, as I love it now. He sent money and boat tickets back to Russia so his fiancé could join him. I really don't know what to believe about the story that followed, but it was told that when he went to the dock to greet his bride-to-be, her older sister walked off the boat. It seems in Russian Jewish culture, daughters were to wed based on their position in the family. A younger sister could not wed until all older sisters were wed. Since my grandfather's fiancé had an unwed older sister, she should be his choice of wife, so that's who the family sent. It's hard to believe that was just a little over 100 years ago.

Whatever the truth is, the two wed and had three sons, my father Jacob being the oldest, born in 1913 in Boston, Massachusetts.

My mother, Sylvia, was born in Louisville Kentucky in 1915. Her father, Joseph Levin, was born in Pennsylvania and her mother, Rose Cohen, was born in Moscow, Russia prior to her parents moving to the U.S. Joseph's parents were both from Belarus. Joe and Rose were married in 1912 in Louisville and my mother Sylvia was their first-born daughter of six children. We don't know how Joe and Rose met—perhaps because both of their parents had emigrated from Russia. Rose never said much, and I only recently realized that English was not her first language. Besides my mother, they had five more children: three boys and three girls total. Two of their sons would fight in World War II.

So what does all this have to do with me? My experience was that I was born into a perfectly normal middle-class Jewish American family with a father that had a good job and a stay-at-home mom who took care of her three sons. My parents bought all their homes and were upwardly mobile. They managed a newspaper branch out of our garage to make a little extra money, and I would hang out with the older kids who came to pick up their papers to deliver them to their customers. The family started a softball team in their newspaper branch league and we played games every summer weekend with the other branches. We named our team the "Red Devils." My dad designed a team logo and cut a stencil to print the logo on t-shirts we wore to games as our uniforms. He taught me how to stencil on fabric, and how to work in wood. My dad loved working in wood. I still have the carving knives he fashioned by hand out of hand forged steel and handcrafted handles, each with his initials carefully carved into the base of each handle.

My mother's artistic nature would wait to fully bloom

until her children were a bit older. Without much forewarning, she suddenly packed a bag, flew to Chicago, and attended
a florist training program. She opened a shop in our basement
when she got back and started decorating for bar and bat
mitzvahs, weddings, and funerals for the Jewish community.
Dad designed and fabricated floral stands and Chuppahs for
the bride and groom to stand under, and Mom did all the
floral design and arranging. They fought like cats and dogs
through it all (both eldest children, liking to be in control),
but then that happened with everything they did together. We
called them the bickerers. I was the youngest, so I was forced
into indentured servitude in Mom's floral business. I still
know how to make a wicked good topiary tree.

It was the 1950s and early 1960s post-World War II, and
the middle-class was thriving. Life was simple and it was
good. TV's were just being commercialized and my Grandpa
Joe bought three of them and gave us one. It had a fuzzy
nine-inch black and white screen in an enormous cabinet.
There were two channels and four shows per week. We would
gather in the downstairs playroom in front of that tiny screen,
and Dad would peel oranges for us without breaking the
long curly peels he would create. It was magical. My brothers
and I were in school and we were all thriving. All of our
beloofs were firmly in place and functioning perfectly, just
as designed. It was the time of "Father Knows Best" and
"Leave it to Beaver." In our "happy home" nothing more was
ever uttered about the war, the tattoos, or the genocide. I have
no memory of ever visiting with my father's brother Morris
after he left our home.

# 9

# A Word on Shock

I apologize for placing these images here. They are abhorrent to me and make my stomach turn in nausea and disgust. They represent the depths to which man's inhumanity to humankind can slip. I am firmly committed to my new belief that I am not a victim, and there are no other victims either. I am one hundred percent responsible for my life, and I hold others to be one hundred percent responsible for their lives. I believe that life is difficult and we are all here to learn to overcome difficulty. I believe that it is our suffering that develops us into the people we are meant to be. I try to teach these simple spiritual constructs to my clients so that they might be empowered to recover and change.

It's not as if there are no similarly abhorrent and disgusting images of atrocities and genocide taking place daily that we see in live feeds in today's world. We have become so desensitized to violent death and carnage that it hardly affects us anymore. It's what we must do to survive. In my world of healing trauma, we name this process of detaching from our feelings to survive as "shock." It is during our experience of shock that we form our deepest beloofs.

I first saw these images on a large white projection screen standing on the pulpit of our family's synagogue when I was perhaps four or five years old. This photo shows the face of shock. The Jewish Community would gather at the Synagogue every year at the time of Yom  HaShoah: Holocaust Remembrance Day. "Never forget," the Rabbi said loudly. "Never forget!" I stood in the back row of seats frozen.

I heard nothing. I felt nothing. I gazed without blinking at these pictures, unable to look away. The overwhelm sent me directly out of my body to somewhere I thought would provide me safety. There was none. There was no model of healing here—only anger, and grief, and fear. So I went away into shock, overwhelmed with emotion that lodged in my body—tucked safely away until one of those damned sessions at Wellness.

Shock is a type of disassociation that separates us from our emotional experiences of the events in our lives. It is perhaps the most important survival mechanism humans possess. It is the process that allows a fireman to run into a burning building to rescue a child, or a soldier to kill the enemy before he is killed, or a therapist to hear the most horrendous of human experiences like sexual abuse, or cult brainwashing without being overcome by emotional trauma herself. It allows us to survive war, or domestic violence, or even genocide without going crazy. Those who do not possess adequate shock protection may experience physical disease, mental illness, or death. Shock is a necessary part of our ability to tolerate the intolerable, to survive the un-survivable.

At the same time, shock is extremely contagious—it spreads like the flu. If we are in a vulnerable state we can "catch" shock from those around us without even knowing it. Young children are especially vulnerable to contagious shock since the adults around them are not conscious of the effects they are having on them. What is clear to me now is that the Rabbi was deep in shock, as was our congregation, as was the entire world Jewish population.

Unfortunately, shock turns into chronic Post Traumatic Stress that can be triggered by even the most unrelated event and turn us from one person into another: enter road rage, domestic abuse, sexual abuse, homicide, suicide, panic attacks, sleep disturbance, depression, anxiety…. So many times we hear people say, "He seemed to be so quiet and reserved…no one would have ever believed he could do such a thing." I believe the increase in police violence upon civilians is a direct result of police departments hiring veterans of our military forces without understanding that PTSD lurks in everyone even peripherally connected to the military. Over the last 5-10 years we have learned how to treat shock and PTSD. As I learned to heal my own shock, it prepared me for what was to come next. There was even deeper trauma to heal. It would begin as a lucid dream I would have in the middle of the night at Wellness.

# 10

# Prelude to the Dachau Experience

I awakened one night in the darkness during my second year at the Wellness Institute. I slept with the other men in a dormitory style room called the "Old Temple" at the Institute. It had been the original teaching room before they built a brand new "Temple" along with sleeping accommodations for over 40 students at a time. It was not uncommon for me to wake up during the night during training weekends, sometimes for a late bathroom break, and sometimes as a result of the work we were doing there. At times, I would write in my journal, or record a dream.

Carl Jung differentiated light consciousness from darkness consciousness. My teacher David would say, "As therapists we are little more than ushers in a movie theater. We shine just enough light to help people find their seats and help them to sit down. We ask them to be quiet and not disturb other's experiences. Everything they need to heal is contained in the symbols of the movie of their lives."

Jung teaches that the messages from the dark time usually appear in symbols that we must decode. The decoding goes on throughout our lives as we move through the progressive developmental stages we experience. We can either become conscious of the meaning of these symbols, or remain asleep for our entire life. I found my writing in the middle of the night to be completely different from my daytime writing. It was lucid and poetic.

But on this particular night, my eyes opened spontaneously and fell on a complete scene of a completely different place. I looked around and saw a very large room with very high ceilings. I knew I was not dreaming because I was still in my bed, but the room had changed right in front of me. There were hundreds if not thousands of people standing on platforms in front of train cars that trailed off into the distant darkness.

This picture is reminiscent of the train station I found myself in that night. Although it is a picture of one of the train stations now in ruins where the Nazis gathered up Jews for the trip to the nearest death chambers, we can imagine it as it was then, brimming with families staring blankly at the platform below, some shrieking as their wives and children were separated out, sometimes children from their mothers. This is what I awakened to.

I wasn't looking at the scene: I was in it. It was not a dream. It was my reality. I was in my current body, lying in my bed. I was not in a different body; I knew what it felt like to be in a different body from the past life experiences I had during breath work. I had never experienced this before. I smelled the bodies of the throngs of people crushed together before me. I smelled the coal burning in the steam engines that would take them to their destiny. I felt their despair and their terror. I was being prepared, and did not want to be. I panicked.

I jumped up from my bed, unable to catch my breath. I ran from the dorm room, through the kitchen, down the stairs and into the large Temple room. Everyone was asleep in their rooms, and it was dark in the Temple except for the filtered light illuminating the packed altar. My heart was pounding out of my chest with panic and at the same time I felt desolate and hopeless. I fell first to my knees, and quickly dropped prostrate on my stomach. I gazed at the large collection of spiritual objects standing in front of me on the three-tiered altar, almost 20 feet wide. Along with all the pieces of art given to the Institute and the pictures of members of the community who had passed, large bronze Hindu Murtis and other spiritual artifacts looked down on my prone body—Saraswati, the Hindu goddess of knowledge, music, arts, wisdom and learning; the upside-down dancing Shiva representing ultimate freedom; and the elephant-headed Ganesh, whose spiritual name Diane had given me years earlier channeled from her teacher Karunamayi. Ganesh is revered as the remover of obstacles, the patron of arts and sciences and the carrier of intellect and wisdom. All of these representations of the aspects of the Creator surrounded me, trying their best to embrace me if I would only allow it.

"Take me away from all of this suffering," I screamed out in my mind. "I don't want to do this anymore! I don't want to be here any longer! This is too difficult…take me now…take me away."

I recalled that once, years earlier, I sat on my bed with a loaded gun in my hands contemplating taking my life after I had lost every worldly possession I acquired during my lifetime—deciding that my family needed my life insurance money more than me. Back then, I was completely over-whelmed with self-loathing. I knew intimately the depression that could bring one to the edge of taking his own life.

But on this night, in my deepest despair, it proves to be different. As I look over the collection of spiritual archetypes before me, my eyes fall upon a depiction of Christ. Reflexively, I look away. "You can't help me, you are a false God. They told me that long ago in Sunday School." But as I continue to gaze upon the image of Christ, and then back to Shiva, and then on to Saraswati, and finally to Ganesh, the teaching becomes crystal clear: "We are all here, and we have always been here. We are simply human's depiction of the aspects of the one universal Creator, the Mystery beyond all Mysteries that resides in your heart since your soul first came into your body. We never abandoned you, even when you had to leave your body to survive. We helped you through until you could become conscious again. You are simply becoming conscious again. You don't have to leave anymore. You are strong enough now and have brought teachers into your life you can trust to show you the way. You have much work left to do—to teach and raise your children, to help your wife and family, to become the teacher you came here to be.

To teach peace.

To teach peace.

You are ready.

# 11
# The Origin of my Beloofs

We are deep into our second year of study at Wellness. We are learning and practicing Psychodrama in Trance. Psychodrama without trance was developed by Jacob L. and Zerka Moreno in the 1940s. Based on the theater model of actors and directors, the Morenos found an effective and experiential mechanism for people to work through their issues by having them participate in live stage plays with the client as the protagonist and the group members as the "players," all guided by experienced psychodrama "directors" (therapists). Psychodrama is very dynamic and effective. Mary Anne and I had the amazing privilege to learn Psychodrama in New York in the 1970s from Zerka herself.

Then in the early 2000s we were treated to relearning Psychodrama at the Wellness Institute with the added feature of trance work. Imagine being the protagonist in your own Psychodrama while you are in trance. Psychodrama on steroids.

In my own Psychodrama that particular weekend I found myself back in the womb again, but now all my characters were present in my energy field; my overwhelmed frenetic mother, my repressed disconnected father, my oldest brother traumatized and angry, my middle brother, weak and manipulative. And of course, there was the rest of my extended family of aunts, uncles, grandparents and cousins; my father's family emotionally and physically absent; and my mother's family— loud, angry, and neurotic.

The stage was set…Lights, camera, ACTION!

Before long, my therapist is down on the mat with me as I try to bury my face into the vinyl covered foam, curl into a fetal position, and hide. The other members of my "cast" are all around me, saying their lines as a cacophony of chaos. What else could I expect; it is a post-Holocaust ancestral cluster fuck. I'm not even born, and yet I am completely overwhelmed and anxious. I feel vulnerable and unsafe.

"What are you are concluding here?" the psychodrama director asks quietly.

I'm quiet for a moment as I try to drop down out of the shock I am experiencing and into my feelings.

"I'm FUCKED!" I reply in a loud whisper. "They don't have a clue who I am and what I need. They are all freaked out! They don't even know how to take care of themselves. I'm trapped in this insanity."

"So what do you decide to do?"

Decide? I'm deciding something? It comes to me immediately. "The only thing I can decide—I have to figure this whole thing out on my own. There is no one here who can help me."

"How do you choose to behave?" she continues.

Choose to behave! I'm trapped in this womb. I have no choice.

"I suck it up and go quiet. I start trying to help everybody else out—perhaps they'll return the favor without my asking. When that doesn't work, I just disconnect from having any needs of my own." I'm surprised this tiny unborn being has figured out so much already; his beloofs.

My cognitive being lights up. In a nanosecond I integrate that these beloofs have governed all of my life, and until this moment of consciousness in my psychodrama, they have operated in the background of every decision I have made. A series of dots begin to connect that become the outline of my entire life until now.

Suddenly, pillows are being piled high on my body. I'm completely encased. A person climbs on top of the pillows covering me.

I can handle this.

Then another climbs on.

No big deal.

Then another and I feel myself unable to breathe.

Another and I'm being crushed underneath the weight. The heat is unbearable. The director's voice whispers in my ear, "How are you doing?"

"I'm fucking dying in here!" I croak.

"What are you going to do?" she yells.

"Let me out of here!" The scream from my body shocks me.

"You have to get yourself out," she says.

I begin to squirm and fight. I am using all of my physical strength to liberate myself. I am kicking and punching and screaming and bucking until I have pushed everything and everyone off me.

I lie there breathing hard, drenched in sweat, but feeling cool air on my body. My breathing starts to calm down and feelings of peace and tranquility begin to flow through me. I remember this is not how it went back then. I was a drugged dead fish that was pulled out numb and asleep. But this is how it went on this day in my psychodrama, and every cell in my body and being is awake and alive.

I breathe the entire experience into every muscle, every cell, every atom, and even the empty spaces in between the atoms of my being. And then I burst into tears, overwhelmed by the depth of grief these beloofs have created ever since my soul entered my body as a simple clump of cells in my mother's womb. But now I know the difference. The difference is in my conscious being. I can adopt new beliefs and decisions. I have the rest of my life to integrate new ways.

# 12

# Dachau: The Beginning of the Split

L ess than 24 hours later we are all back in the Temple room for breath work. Lying there on our mats always reminds me of pre-school nap time—graham crackers and a small carton of milk before lying down, ostensibly to sleep. I never do.

In breath work, we invite our demons to come out of the darkness of the sub-conscious mind into the light of consciousness for healing. Carl Jung spoke volumes on the subject. Mary Anne teaches in our PTI groups about how the darkness of our shadow parts is formed during trauma to protect the tiny child within us. So those parts that lurk in the shadows are very young themselves. When we become conscious of what lurks in the shadows, we discover our "silver platters:" our deepest pain and injuries are exposed so that they can heal. No one enjoys the discovery of their silver platters and I am no different. But I know that they come to us on the road to enlightenment.

Today I am about to discover perhaps the most terrifying, overwhelming silver platter one can imagine.

I really don't care if you do or don't believe in past lives, or Karma, or attachments, or entities, or anything else for that matter. And I'm definitely not preaching that you should. You may judge what I am about to describe as "clinically absurd" (one psychiatrist's assessment of a client of mine recalling her birth experience in detail), psychotic, weird, woo-woo, amazing, or impossible. You may decide what I am about to share with you is real, or unreal, fact or fiction. You can believe that my mind tricked me into creating what I experienced from the pictures I saw in the Synagogue that day when I was so young, or that my soul inhabited a being that was there before it came here. It really doesn't matter. It is simply my experience, lying on a mat at the Wellness Institute that day and nothing more.

Also, I do not intend to vilify or blame the Germans or the rest of the world for allowing the Holocaust to happen. It had nothing to do with me personally, and I don't consider myself or my Jewish tribe to be victims. I accept that human beings have been murdering each other since they came to be. My Buddhist nature knows that without suffering we may not know joy. However, I can choose to suffer or to heal in my own life.

As always, the memories start in my body and move into consciousness. Breathing, rocking, breathing, rocking, dropping and tantrum-ing, flipping onto my back and continuing to breathe. After my difficult psychodrama just a day before, I say a little prayer to the breath work Gods to be gentle. That may have been my mistake.

Over the next 90 minutes, I am transported into the body of another person in another time, first enjoying the bounty of his wonderful life and family,  to being kidnapped as a prisoner torn from his family, to turning over all of his worldly goods to an army of haters, to being herded naked into a courtyard outside the "showers" they were asked to take, to gasping his last breath in the back corner of a large brick room along with hundreds of other men, women, and children.

Breathing on my mat, coughing first—maybe a little cold coming on—then gasping and coughing, my body retreating back up against the wall of the Temple of Wellness. But it's not the wall of Wellness anymore. It is brick and cold. I'm trying to break through the wall to the other side where there is fresh air to breathe.

I am only there now…pressing our mouth and face into the brick wall as we desperately try not to breathe in the Zyklon B pesticide used to exterminate over one million Jews at Auschwitz alone. The wall does not breathe for us, and we begin dying together. The shock and terror of our impending death is overwhelming, suffocating as the air in our lungs is replaced with the awful tasting gas robbing our cells of the oxygen they need to live, gasping, arms flailing, legs pushing until our body finally relaxes into death.

I know exactly where I am. I am not in this life, not in Rob's body. I don't even know our name in this other life, the life I had just before this one. But I know who I was, a successful businessman, wealthy in fact, with a wife and grown children. My wife had fled earlier with my children to America. She begged me to come. I scoffed at her. Naive girl, my inflated ego said. Don't be silly. These people are crackpots and fascists. Our society will protect us. The world will save us. They will never succeed. I am not going to give up everything I have ever worked for and leave it behind. Go to America with the children. You can come home when this is all over. I'll stay and protect what we have built here.

History would prove him wrong. In this other life, so many of us would die an excruciating death, never to see our families again, taking with us overwhelming shame, guilt, and horror, again to conclude we are a fuck-up, defective, wrong. I will bring with me into this life a hint of the ghost of his ego; his need to show the world his wealth, power, achievement, and success—all to disprove his deep feelings of inadequacy. Since this ego is intact at his death, I will need at least another lifetime—this lifetime—to try to heal it. And perhaps more lifetimes if I cannot complete the healing work in this one. I make a pact with myself to try my best.

Unfortunately, I will find later that I also brought an attachment even bigger needing to be released—hundreds of silver platters. But for now, it's enough. I come back from my breath work letting myself rest and integrate. I know there is more to come later.

So, if you find my experience unbelievable and judge it to be a fabrication of my Steven Spielberg brain, riddle me this: if you must believe this is not a past life experience brought to consciousness for healing, but rather some other phenomenon, why would one choose to put himself through such an ordeal lying on a mat at a retreat center in Issaquah Washington when he could have just had a nice graham cracker and milk, and taken a restful nap?

# 13

# Ego

Since birth, I've always fast-tracked myself. The third of three boys, I always wanted to do what my brothers were doing. I copied them. My oldest brother Alan loved me unconditionally, and enjoyed teaching and mentoring me. When one or the other of my parents was physically violent toward me, he would deflect their abuse onto himself. My middle brother Michael was always in competition with me and resented my presence. He always needed to be the center of attention and had difficulty sharing. He always found someone else to blame for what was happening in his life. He never learned to love.

Alan passed away in April, 2012 at the age of 69—too young. He was diabetic and had coronary artery disease. Throughout his life, I had admonished him to eat right and exercise regularly. When he was visiting once, I bought him a pair of running shoes. I don't think they ever left the box. I miss him painfully.

Michael has not spoken to me since August, 1995 at my mother's funeral. My father died in 1992 of lung cancer, so she was the last parent to leave. Since then, I've forgotten that I have another living brother. I don't know if he ever really attached to me, or me to him. It goes that way sometimes. I know when I think of him, I feel love for him. I can't have a relationship with him, but I can keep doing my work around him.

At four, I cried when my two brothers went off to school and I could not. So my mother let me go to the daycare center down the street a few mornings a week so I could have some fun and she could have a break too. My beloofs were totally operant: when the bully at the day care cornered me behind the piano and hit me in the face, I told no one. I sucked it up and stayed quiet. I knew I had to figure it out on my own—that no one could help me. Remember? I figured all that out before I left the womb.

I went to a private school for first grade at five, too young to go to the public school. It was wonderful! Housed in a church with two loving teachers, one older and one younger for the twenty-four kids in my class. They knew how to make learning fun and natural. Then at six, I went on to public school for second grade since my parents could not afford the private school any longer. Thirty-five kids with one teacher in a huge brick building. I was one year younger than all the other kids in my class.

No one told me where the bathroom was. I sat in the back of the room, the teacher not knowing I hadn't been there for first grade. I kept sitting, waiting for a time to go to the bathroom. Squirming in my chair, I knew I had to pee. Again, I told no one. Not knowing what to do, I peed right there in my chair. I had gone deep into shock: a familiar place. I sucked it up and stayed quiet. I knew I had to figure it out on my own—that no one could help me. Remember? I figured all that out before I left the womb. My beloofs had become my operating system.

That's how my own personal beloofs operated early in my life. My beloofs are as unique and as personal as my unique spirit. They are my personal creation. It's important that each of us discover our own beloofs and how they were born. That is the secret of how our hypnotherapy processes are so effective.

Our beloofs develop during our most formative experiences to protect us during times of struggle, and then reside silently in our subconscious mind doing their job. They are quite necessary for our survival when trauma befalls us, and trauma befalls us all as we develop. That's right; no one is immune from trauma and struggle. The simple fact that our soul decides comes to earth and enter a body starts the process. We start to develop our own personal ego as we learn about our world and how we fit into it. It is this ego development that forms our beloofs. A kid beats me up behind the piano at pre-school and I already know how to suck it up and survive.

Then in my new second grade classroom, I have to pee and the same beloofs govern that situation; only, this time it results in confusion, shame, and embarrassment. As she carefully leads me from the classroom crying, my teacher gives me an option—"Next time, please let me know when you need to go to the bathroom and I'll show you where to go."

What she fails to realize is that the shame I feel only drives the beloof deeper. While I now know where to go to the bathroom, I feel like a bigger fuck-up than I felt before. And now I have to hide it even deeper down inside of me. I still don't know about the young Revolutionary War soldier, his death as a coward and a deserter at the hands of his comrades, and his personal visit with his creator in the inter-life. Those beloofs will remain dormant as attachments until the larger struggles during my adult life erupt—when my ego cracks wide open under their weight.

# 14

# Setting Up for Our Children's Beginning

Mary Anne and I lived together in a "duplex" in Dayton Ohio after graduating from the University of Michigan in 1973. We were back to fulfill a commitment to the State of Ohio Department of Children's Services after we both applied for and received a scholarship and stipend to study for our Master's degrees.

That same year we survived the death of both of Mary Anne's parents, just eight months apart. Mary Anne was 26. Her mother died in the recovery room after having one of the first heart bypass surgeries ever done. Her hard life and cigarettes and coffee caught up with her, and she just didn't want to live with the pain anymore. She was willing to take the risk. Her father died eight months later of his broken heart, although kidney failure would be the cause of death on his death certificate. He was 83, and had fought in World War I as a naval seaman. He was a consummately private man and most likely suffered from PTSD. We found out after both had died that Peg, Mary Anne's mother, was his second wife. He left his divorce papers on top of his belonging in his private trunk. He had his children with Peg after the age of 52.

Mary Anne and I were seated in the waiting room after deciding with the doctor not to do a very risky procedure to try to save her father. There was a high probability that the procedure would kill him, and Mary Anne had already been through that with her mother. It was a decision no 26 year old should be faced with. Unexpectedly, the nurse came to tell me that Al called me to come alone into his hospital room. I had no idea why. I was that Jewish kid his daughter was shacked up with; what could he want to talk to me about?

When I went into his darkened room he drew me close and said, "I want you to promise me something."

"What's that?" I replied.

"I want you to promise me that you will always take care of Mary Anne."

Jesus, I thought, Mary Anne and I are fanatic feminists and Gloria Steinem is our hero. I'm not supposed to take care of Mary Anne as she is quite capable of taking care of herself, and she wouldn't let me under any circumstances anyway. She graduated from high school second in her class, was a summa cum laude and Phi Beta Kappa graduate of Ohio University, and just received her Master of Social Work from the University of Michigan. No one in her family even came close to accomplishing what she had accomplished. I squeaked out of undergraduate school hung over with a 2.8 cumulative average, and had to talk the Dean of the University of Michigan School of Social Work into giving me a chance to attend graduate school there after having been refused admission. If anyone was taking care of anyone, it was her taking care of me.

"I promise, Al," I said in a whisper. "I will always take care of your daughter." I had never been that close to someone who was passing, and his sense of calm calmed me.

"Don't ever forget your promise to me and don't ever tell her I said this."

"I won't forget and I will never tell her."

I did not share with him that Mary Anne and I made a promise to always tell each other the truth and to keep no secrets from each other. It wasn't important for him to know.

Al drifted back into his medication fog and I quietly left the room and returned to Mary Anne in the waiting room.

"You're father just made me promise to always take care of you and to never tell you he told me that," I blurted.

"That's just like him," she said adamantly, her irritation just covering her deep sadness and grief. "I'm glad you told me. I don't want you to carry that pressure."

After we left the hospital that night and went home to get some sleep, Mary Anne's father passed. We were awakened in the middle of the night to a phone call with the news, and cried in each other's arms. And even though Mary Anne has always given me permission not to take care of her, I've kept my promise to Al. It was a promise not of obligation, but of love. Mary Anne has been my soul mate, my sister, my wife, the mother of my children and my closest friend. I don't know what will be harder: to leave her here alone when I leave this life, or to be left alone when she leaves this life. I live each day trying not to think about that.

Mary Anne left me for a time after her parents died. On the surface, she said she didn't think I was the right partner for her. In retrospect, she was right. I had a controlling tyrannical shadow that rivaled my mother's. Sometimes it still rears its ugly head. Back then, I thought it was my personal power and my right. But that shadow was based in the beloofs I created to protect my fears of abandonment and scarcity. I was not aware of those shadows at the time. They lurked deep in my subconscious mind and in the beloofs birthed in the bowels of the Holocaust and the past life of the German Jew who died in the gas chamber.

Mary Anne was in deep shock following the death of her parents and had to heal herself from such an early and complete loss. When she left me, I was devastated. But although it was deeply painful for me to endure and reflect upon, I needed to know that I could make it without her and not take her leaving personally. That's hard to do when the person you love most dearly in life must move on, no matter what the reason. Later we learned to fully embrace the belief that "what other people think of me is none of my business."

Dealing with that truth so young has been a lifelong asset to me. It allows me to love unconditionally: Mary Anne, my children, my extended family, and everyone I come in contact with. What others think of me is none of my business—priceless.

Thankfully, our relationship was not to be denied, and after some months of living apart, and a lot of good therapy, we re-committed to our relationship and began a life of marriage. Although Mary Anne was raised in a liberal Christian home, she never really bought into the "Jesus son of God thing" as she put it. She had become interested in Judaism in college and decided to formalize her conversion to become a Jew by choice. I've always chided her that she got to choose Judaism as an adult while I was born into it. Her devotion and love of my own religion has proven to be an inspiration to me to stay connected to it.

But this period would prove not to be the end of my ego shadow, simply my introduction to it. What I perceived to be success and achievement came around to bite me in the butt, just like my predecessor who died in the gas chamber.

# 15
# We Move to Seattle

Everything is going smashingly. Mary Anne and I buy our first house in Dayton a year before we marry on September 12, 1976. I am 26 years old, and already the director of a small decentralized mental health center in a suburb of Dayton called Trotwood. Mary Anne is a mental health therapist in a large metropolitan hospital. My beloofs about achieving recognized status and financial comfort are in high gear. I am the youngest director in the county, perhaps the whole state. Mary Anne is fully on board as our thirst for acquisition and status grows.

The country is in the midst of the social programs started by John F. Kennedy and expanded by Lyndon B. Johnson. We somehow survived the tumult of the 1960s race riots and the assassinations of John, Martin, and Bobby, and Ronald Reagan had not yet arrived to dismantle the social programs that the Democrats had built. The mental health system is flourishing and effective. The long-term mental hospitals have been emptied and closed with the advent of more effective psychotropic drugs and out-patient psychotherapy services. We are keeping the mental health patients treated and out of the criminal justice system. The economy is flourishing and the middle class is strong and vibrant.

But I want more, and Mary Anne wants out of Dayton. My whole family lives within 200 miles of each other in Ohio and Kentucky and it's difficult to leave. But we are also intuitively aware that Ohio is too conservative for us, and we lust for a more affluent and exciting lifestyle. I am quite clear that I want to be in private practice since I had grown up with entrepreneurs on both sides of my family, and, of course, the most successful and admirable mental health professionals are in private practice. We are being called to both coasts, as we love beautiful country and coastal water. Ohio has neither, consisting mostly of cornfields and manufacturing complexes.

A colleague of Mary Anne's who grew up in Washington State implored us to visit the Northwest before we made any decision about where we would settle down to start our own practice and perhaps a family. In August of 1977 we take a three-week vacation and fly to Seattle. We stay with acquaintances in the foothills of the Cascade Range, to the east of Seattle and near beautiful Lake Sammamish...and then with friends on Bainbridge Island, across Puget Sound from Seattle. I stood on the bow of a ferry during one of our many rides from Seattle to Bainbridge looking at a view very similar to this one, when I turned to Mary Anne and said, "We would be crazy not to move here." When we returned from our vacation, we let our friends and family know we decided to move to Seattle. Everyone was sure we had gone off the deep end, and that our delusion would pass.

But we put our house up for sale, sold it in two weeks, packed all or our belongings in a 22-foot Ryder truck, and in November of 1977, just over one year after our wedding, we "trucked" out west with our dog Sunny. Everyone was in tears by our departure—my parents, Mary Anne's brother (one tagged along with us), all of our extended family and our close friends. In the decades we have lived here, we have never regretted the decision.

We had no jobs when we arrived, and Seattle was just recovering from a serious recession. The real estate market was sizzling and the social service jobs we were seeing paid very little. My goal to start a private practice was alive and well, but we needed quick income. We both took a three-week training program to get our real estate licenses and went to work for a small company run by an ex social service director. He had hired a rag-tag group of out-of-work social workers in a hot real estate market. He believed social workers had the "empathy" necessary to sell houses. We met one of our first friends in Seattle: Frank. He had come from Michigan to settle into the gay-friendly community here. We became immediate and fast friends, selling houses and partying together. By 1984, Mary Anne and I would have two children, and Frank would have died as one of the very first casualties of the AIDS epidemic that had reached the U.S. in the early 1980s. His quick illness and death shocked and saddened us. We had never lost a peer before.

The beloofs I had formed early in this life regarding achievement and success were paying off big time, and I seemed to be creating success and recognition at every turn. But the underlying beloofs I brought to this life about being a fuck-up, and the beloofs I created in the womb about having to suck up my feelings and do it all on my own continued to operate at an unconscious and core level. On the outside, I appeared in total control, while on the inside I suffered from daily panic and isolation. I felt like a complete and utter fraud.

We lived beyond our means, using the equity in our houses to fund a more extravagant lifestyle than we could afford. My parent's "helped" us out financially to afford nicer houses in more expensive neighborhoods. In 1987, when my oldest daughter was six and my younger daughter was three, we moved into a large home on Mercer Island, Washington. Mercer Island just happened to be the most expensive zip code in the state. Ostensibly we had moved there because the schools were so highly rated. My parents helped us to place both our children in an expensive private Jewish Day School that we could not afford on our own. Again, they wanted to "help." We joined the Beach Club down the street, vacationed in Oregon and Hawaii on a regular basis, and ran with doctors, lawyers, and successful entrepreneurs. By the time we entered the 1990s, I was a raging workaholic and money addict. My college days of alcohol and pot gave way to the more socially acceptable addictions to work, money, and status. Still no conscious word from my sleeping, past-life experiences and their attendant beloofs.

My anxiety grew more acute, and my beloof that I was a fraud was driving the bus. I was operating in the shadows of self-sabotage and psychic destruction. My Lear Jet was flying a course directly into a mountainside and I had no working warning equipment. Mary Anne and I would learn in just a few short years how important the call to Seattle was for us.

# 16
# Cruising Altitude

I was working way too many hours trying to maintain the lifestyle we had created raising our children in an advantaged neighborhood with values that reflected my beloofs rather than my soul. Money and status were King, and how I achieved it was secondary. Mercer Island was populated with conservative old money—families holding generations of wealth. Many of its residents were born into the wealth of their ancestors or created their own wealth in wealth-producing industries. Few had been born into the Holocaust families I grew up with in Dayton, Ohio. I was quickly caught up in comparing myself to them and competing with them, having chosen a career of service and healing. I was running with doctors and lawyers and technology entrepreneurs. Like my family of origin, I didn't realize they just didn't get me.

We joined an upper middle-class Mercer Island synagogue where our children were named and later celebrated their Bat Mitzvahs. We attended a few services during the year and every High Holiday Service in the fall. Every year in the fall at the time of the High Holy Days, the men would go to the Synagogue to move the pulpit to the other end of the social hall and set up temporary seating. It was the only way all the "three-day Jews" who attended only the High Holy Day services could be accommodated. The Synagogue had contracted with the Boeing Airplane Company years ago to build them a "Bimah" (pulpit) that was outfitted with air cushions that would inflate just like the ones Boeing used to move airplane sections around the manufacturing floor. The Bimah was so huge it could not be moved any other way. Like many other religions, you had to be seen on the most holy of days even though you did not attend the rest of the year.

I always felt weird being a three-day Jew. I felt little connection to the prayers and the ritual, although I still knew it all from memory (not heart) and could chant the prayers without referring to the prayer book. I also felt little connection to the other three-day Jews I saw there, although we made sure to spend time catching up on our kids' accomplishments and our personal achievements. I was recreating the life of my parents and the concentration camp man without knowing it, just as he had most likely done; laboring under the same unconscious beloofs I carried within me.

As my children were growing into adolescence, a volcano was brewing deep inside of me just under the surface that had been stirred to life in the form of my firstborn daughter, Jessica. First she, and then her younger sister Liz, would prove to be my strongest teachers and spirit guides of this lifetime. Without knowing it, just by living their own Karma, they would reintroduce me to my own personal Higher Power and my soul. I never guessed this would be the case.

Jessica came into this world first on January 14, 1981. She didn't start breathing right away after the 24-hour labor under the drug-induced contractions she and Mary Anne had been subjected to. It was the standard Pitocin protocol when the mother's water breaks but contractions have not started. I sat and breathed with Mary Anne through every contraction during that 24-hour period. About 22 hours into the labor, having not complained once, Mary Anne called me close to her much like her father did just before he passed.

She uttered softly, "I don't think I can do this."

Mary Anne's perfectionism and suffering in silence be-loofs were hard at work. I knew them well and knew what to do.

I immediately turned to the nurse who sat with us throughout the labor to monitor the Pitocin drip. "She needs medication now," I said calmly. She looked up from the book she was reading, looked at Mary Anne, who looked no different than she had 22 hours ago, and simply said, "She seems OK to me."

"She just told me she doesn't think she can do this," I said to the nurse, now with a slight edge to my voice.

"I didn't hear her say anything," she retorted.

This woman was about to meet my warrior shadow.

"She needs meds, now!" I insisted. The edge to my voice changed to a rumble and echoed slightly against the walls of the room.

"I'll get the doctor in right away," the nurse said as she ran from the room.

The magma started to recede a bit.

The doctor came, placed a saddle block into Mary Anne's back with a very large, long menacing needle, and I could feel her relax. Jessica arrived without a sound about 90 minutes later. Mary Anne and I stopped breathing until we heard Jessica's faint cry from the other side of the room. Years later, when Jessica would have her first hypnotherapy session with our teacher Diane, she would return to that room and re-experience her breathless birth. She would tell the story about how she labored to begin breathing and no one seemed to be able to help her. She re-experienced seeing a doctor who came over to where she lay. She said, "When I saw him, I knew he would be able to start me breathing." He was perhaps the first of her angels in this life. Thank God she has had many more along the way.

One of Jessica's first teachings for me was just a few minutes later when they laid her on Mary Anne's stomach. Her eyes were open and she locked on to Mary Anne's eyes immediately. They say that newborns can't focus at first, but what I saw in Jessica's eyes proved otherwise. As I looked at Jessica greeting her mother for the first time on the outside, I heard my own voice saying internally, "Oh my God, she is a complete and independent human being. She has everything within her to live her life the way she wishes, both good and bad."

I was terrified.

I carried many of the unconscious beloofs about being a parent that many of us carry. The beloofs of my own parents, and their parents before them, were programmed into me. That program was activated the moment I looked into Jessica's eyes: the beloof that parents are parents for life, and children are children for life. The beloof that parents must mold and create their children in their own image. If our children choose a path that is different from ours, or we don't believe in, or determine to be dangerous to them, we must teach and guide them to be on the correct path. My ancestry kicked in automatically, unconsciously.

It all worked fine for the first few years. Jessica sought our approval and learned all the appropriate responses to maintain our love and protection. She was a very happy child, curious about everything. She soaked up information and knowledge like a sponge and we were happy to provide it. She played, and drew, and read, and laughed and cried. I thought, "Maybe I can pull this off. She's a good kid and she will always love me. She'll make all the right decisions and make me look like I actually know what I'm doing as a parent." So I sucked up all my self-doubt and stayed quiet. I knew I had to figure it out on my own, that no one could help me. Remember those beloofs? They were still calling the shots from my mother's womb.

What my unconscious parenting beloofs were really saying was, "She will make all the decisions I want her to make, and she will always follow MY lead and MY direction." My inherited ancestral parenting beloofs completely drowned out the memories of my own adolescence. They completely engaged and trumped what my psych professors had taught me in grad school about individuation, adolescence, and authority.

When I turned 15, just two years after being the consummate Bar Mitzvah boy, I created a fake ID that claimed I was 18 years old, and started buying beer at the corner grocery store along with the cigarettes I had been buying since I was 11. I was pissed off and rebellious. I hated school and gave it little effort. I wanted to hang out with my friends, smoke cigarettes, drink beer, and stay out late. They were all a year older than me since I had gone to school a year early, and most of them were already driving. Within a year I had my license and a 1956 Plymouth Savoy my father was going to take to the junkyard as a derelict. I talked him into giving it to me.

Cars back then rusted out from the salt they put down on Ohio streets and roads in winter, and engines were lucky to last 60,000 miles. But my Plymouth was my freedom. I went anywhere and everywhere I wanted in that car. The rocker panels under the driver's door had rusted out, so I could flick ashes from my cigarettes directly onto the roadway below. I was making $1.10 per hour working at the local shoe store with a couple of my friends. I had gas, food, beer, and cigarette money in my pocket and we would hang out at the local pool hall paying sixty cents per hour to rent a pool table. I regularly drove drunk at a time when the local police would pull you over, admonish you not to drink and drive, and send you home to your unconscious parents. My parents had no idea about my lifestyle, or simply did not know what to do about it.

How could I be so shocked then, when I finally became aware of Jessica's acting out in the years shortly after her Bat Mitzvah. How could my beautiful little girl betray me so completely? She was supposed to be different. She wasn't supposed to become an individual; her destiny was to be a clone of the image I projected into the world—didn't she get that? As she escalated her acting out, I escalated my need to control her. As I escalated my need to control her, her need to become an individual kept pace. It soon became a Battle of the Titans, and I was sure to win.

And then at 14, she ran away. She upped the ante and trumped me.

I panicked, afraid for her life. So I tracked her down and whisked her away to a boarding school/treatment center in Montana. Then she ran from there, and was picked up in Idaho by the State Highway Patrol. I had them take her back to the boarding school.

As I cried with Mary Anne in our lonely house, and Jessica's younger sister Liz quietly played by herself deep in the shock of losing her sister, some words from a children's story we had read to both of them came to me, a book called *The Runaway Bunny* by Margaret Wise Brown.

*Once there was a little bunny who wanted to run away. So he said to his mother, "I am running away."*

*"If you run away," said his mother, "I will run after you. For you are my little bunny."*

*"If you run after me," said the little bunny, "I will become a fish in a trout stream and I will swim away from you."*

*"If you become a fish in a trout stream," said his mother, "I will become a fisherman and I will fish for you."*

*"If you become a fisherman," said the little bunny, "I will become a rock on the mountain, high above you."*

*"If you become a rock on the mountain high above me," said his mother, "I will become a mountain climber, and I will climb to where you are."*

*"If you become a mountain climber," said the little bunny, "I will be a crocus in a hidden garden."*

*"If you become a crocus in a hidden garden," said his mother, "I will be a gardener. And I will find you."*

*"If you are a gardener and find me," said the little bunny, "I will be a bird and fly away from you."*

*"If you become a bird and fly away from me," said his mother, "I will be a tree that you come home to."*

*"If you become a tree," said the little bunny, "I will become a little sailboat, and I will sail away from you."*

*"If you become a sailboat and sail away from me," said his mother, "I will become the wind and blow you where I want you to go."*

*"If you become the wind and blow me," said the little bunny, "I will join a circus and fly away on a flying trapeze."*

*"If you go flying on a flying trapeze," said his mother, "I will be a tightrope walker, and I will walk across the air to you."*

*"If you become a tightrope walker and walk across the air,"*

said the little bunny, "I will become a little boy and run into a house."

"If you become a little boy and run into a house," said the mother bunny, "I will become your mother and catch you in my arms and hug you."

"Shucks," said the little bunny, "I might just as well stay where I am and be your little bunny."

And so he did.

"Have a carrot," said the mother bunny.

The little bunny knew he had magic and destiny to fulfill, and a mother who knew he was not yet ready.

During the time she was away in Montana, the picture of newborn Jessica looking straight and true into her mother's eyes was still displayed on our refrigerator door. When I gazed again into those clear eyes, I realized I had seen the magic and destiny in them from the moment I met her. In that moment of remembering the runaway bunny, my fears softened a bit, and my parenting beloofs began to defrost, to melt.

Jessica called us a day or two later from the boarding school and said she wanted to come home. The counselors there wanted to escalate the power struggle even further, and advised us to let them make a delinquency filing and send her up the road to a lockup facility. We drove the 10 hours to Montana the next day and picked her up. Liz still looked on in shock, all of her feelings locked up inside, trying to cope.

A few weeks later, Jessica and Mary Anne found an American Eskimo puppy to bring home, and Jessica named him Akiva. She liked the sound of the name, and probably didn't know what it meant. Akiva comes from the Hebrew for "to protect, shelter." It is also a derivative of the name Yakov,

Jacob, my father's and her grandfather's given name. He had passed just a couple of years earlier in 1992.

Akiva was Jessica's "recovery" dog and accompanied her to most of the 12-step meetings she attended in the time that followed. When Jessica was a bit older and working and living out on her own, Akiva became Mary Anne's recovery dog. He lived with us for 16 years and died peacefully at our home one night in 2013, lying in a beanbag chair. May he rest in peace— he helped us all through difficult times.

I started going to Al-Anon meetings shortly after that. Mary Anne had been going to them for some time. While I appreciated the support and advice it provided her, I was different: I could handle it on my own. You know those beloofs by heart by now—say it with me: "So I sucked up all my self-doubt and stayed quiet. I knew I had to figure it out on my own—that no one could help me." Jesus, Rob, you know your beloofs aren't working anymore, give it up. So I took her lead and started attending meetings.

Al-Anon introduced me to some alternative beliefs I could try on for size:

"We admitted we were powerless and our lives had become unmanageable." Powerless? Maybe for you guys, but definitely not me. Unmanageable? I'm John Wayne! "Fill your hands you sons-of-bitches!"

"We came to believe that only a power greater than ourselves could restore us to sanity." Power greater than me? Really? And don't start talking about God to me; he's that scary guy I learned about in Sunday school, and anyway, he abandoned us in the concentration camps.

"We made a decision to turn our will and our lives over to the care of God as we understood God." Did you not hear me? My God abandoned us in the camps. He doesn't exist. Every time I've asked him to show himself to me, he hasn't. Every time I've asked him to answer me, I hear nothing.

At the end of each meeting they said, "Keep coming back; it works if you work it." So I kept going back. Working the 12 steps and hanging out with the "regular" people I met there, I started seeing how my beloofs about being defective, about being alone, about having to figure it out by myself, about how God had abandoned my tribe, about how my children represented an extension of myself, about how if they became their own individual selves they would leave me and I would die alone just like the German Jew in the gas chamber, could be healed by my own personal higher power if I simply relaxed and handed them over to the universe to be transformed.

I was amazed to see that while I belooved I was a fuck-up and defective, I had compensated by seeing myself as better than everyone else and simply entitled to all life had to offer me. I had separated myself fully from any form of a higher power, and in the process, from humankind.

I started to carefully study the 12 steps of Alcoholics Anonymous rather that just read them. As a hypnotherapist, the tools of my trade are contained in the languaging we use to communicate and in our conscious thoughts. Thought is expressed in words and sentences, and within those words and sentences, if we listen very slowly and carefully, we connect and experience each other. It is our primary way of making human connection, and within that connection is our connection to the divine.

I saw that every pronoun in each of the 12 Steps of Alcoholics Anonymous exists in the plural: "We;" "Our;" "Us;" "Ourselves." There is not a single "I" or "Me." I had always prided myself on being unique, different, and special. If I were to be one of the masses, perhaps one day they would come for me again.

I spent an entire year just accepting step one: *"We admitted we were powerless over_____and our lives had become unmanageable."* In my beloof system, powerless meant weak. I cannot be weak. When we are weak, we are killed.

But then I listened more closely to the Serenity Prayer we said as we closed each meeting: *"God, grant me the serenity to accept the things I cannot change, the courage to change the things I can, and the wisdom to know the difference."*

There it was in one simple sentence. The Serenity Prayer would become one of the most important guideposts in my life. That first step didn't mean I had to accept everything in life and that I had no influence or control. It meant I had to learn about powerlessness. I never embraced powerlessness as an asset, and yet knowing the limits of my control and influence allows me to breathe and relax. I learned that most everything in life is out of my hands, especially when it came to my relationships.

So after that first year, I started to study the second of the twelve steps: *"We came to believe that only a power greater than ourselves could restore us to sanity."* Wow, what a sentence. I had to break it down into some parts.

"We came to believe…" Came to believe? I was a 46-year-old man, a respected therapist no less. My beliefs (beloofs?) were the foundation of my life. You don't willy-nilly change your "beliefs." The world would start to wobble on its axis. I treated my beliefs (beloofs) as if they were laws of nature. My sponsor would say, "How's that been working for you?" Shit.

"…that only a power greater than ourselves…" OK, here it comes. You're going to slip the God thing in here on me, and that dog just won't hunt. Our God abandoned us in the camps—remember? I don't want to have anything to do with him. (Him?)

Then, I remembered sitting in on a counseling session with my daughter at the boarding school one winter day in Montana. The counselor asked her, "Do you believe in God?" She quickly answered an emphatic "No!"

I was shocked. She had had her Bat Mitzvah just two years earlier, just like all her friends. It never crossed my mind that day that only three years had passed between the time I was the perfect Bar Mitzvah boy at 13, and the strident 16 year old who ripped the gold Mezuzah from my neck and threw it at my mother yelling, "This is your religion, not mine. Without missing a beat, the counselor said, "It's fine here for you not to believe in God as long as you don't believe that you're God." I could accept that.

"…could restore us to sanity." Restore me to sanity? Seriously? Do I need to remind you that I'm a respected therapist? I'm an expert on sanity.

Then the crazy scenes from the last couple of years started replaying in my mind. The screaming matches, the groundings, words that came out of my mouth that I had promised I would never utter, much less scream at a 14 year old who was just trying to make her way in life, or at my wife who I had promised to love and honor. The words I did not even see going into my quiet and gentle 10-year-old youngest daughter Liz. She was probably just around the corner in the other room out of my view and consciousness, but listening and feeling just the same.

The words I screamed were not the words of my soul; they were the words my mother screamed at my brother Alan. In the shock of the confrontations that had taken place almost

40 years earlier, I recorded them deep in my subconscious mind, only to be triggered in the similar moments that Jessica presented. My soul words would have said, "You are scaring me to death. I have no idea what to do in this situation—I am totally unprepared for this." Had I only known this truth back then.

In my family of origin, I was the youngest, quiet child just around the corner in the other room hearing and witnessing the verbal and physical violence playing out between my mother and oldest brother. In my childhood family, I was Liz. But in my adult family, my mother's parenting beloofs recorded in my subconscious mind became the insanity recreated between me and Jess. My ancestral parenting beloofs were not to be denied. While Jessica and I acted out our drama during her teenage years, the trauma Liz experienced would lie dormant for a few more years, to be worked out in her twenties. It was her struggle and my own fall from grace that would prompt my return to the Wellness Institute in 2003.

OK: insanity it was and is. I get it. Step three.

*"We made a decision to turn our will and our lives over to the care of God as we understood God."* OK, they uttered the word—no fair. My sponsor said, "Calm down—what word can work for you?"

It is said that there are more than 10,000 names for God. Higher Power worked for me back then. Now I like "the Mystery beyond all Mysteries." Why try to put a name on something that is beyond our understanding. When I need one word or two words, I use "Creator," or the First Nation term "Great Spirit."

My work in the 12 Steps of Alcoholics Anonymous reintroduced me to the possibility of recognizing a power greater than myself in my life. My personal work in Heart-Centered Hypnotherapy, Psychodrama in Trance, and Breath Work allowed my relationship with the Mystery beyond all Mysteries to come to life as a living, breathing, visceral experience. I try to grow that relationship through a daily practice of meditation and prayer. Teaching spiritual reconnection has been a major aspect of my own return to sanity.

But I was not quite finished creating insanity in my life to grow even further along my spiritual path. It's the Buddhist way, you know.

# 17

# Flying My Lear Jet into the Mountain

During the last half of the decade of the 1990s, after healing a big piece of my addiction and co-addiction tendencies through my work in the 12-step programs, I returned to cruising altitude. Jessica was back home (mostly), found a niche in the new Flash Internet development community, attended community college classes, and made good money working on a laptop sitting on a couch in our downstairs family room developing websites for high class New York jewelry companies.

It took only a year for Jessica to win worldwide recognition with the newness of Flash and how quickly she discovered its full potential. She produced a Flash version of the game Yahtzee that was picked up by CNet. They asked her to write an article on how she had done it, and that was that. Within a year, she had developed an online Flash community that boasted over 10,000 members with more that 200 developers online at any given time during the day and night. She "moderated" that bulletin board day and night answering questions and teaching Flash. She was known across the globe as the "Flash Goddess."

Between the time she was 18 and 20, Jessica contributed chapters to two Flash tutorial publications, and then authored her own full-length Flash book for an international publisher who had approached her with the project. She moved out of our home with her boyfriend whom she was supporting, (oops) and lived well on her income and her notoriety. But unfortunately, beloofs are like the flu; they are contagious. Jessica would have one or two more crashes to experience before settling down into adulthood.

The shadow Jessica cast both in the easy times and the hard times was long and imposing. She is a big spirit with big energy, and she has always liked working hard and achieving success. It is the spirit of my mother, Sylvia, who was stymied in her family system from expressing herself fully until she was much older. Our "free spirit" approach to raising Jessica allowed her big energy to explode in opposing directions at different times. At times, in self-destructive ways, and at other times, in beautifully creative and productive ways. While Al-Anon finally taught me to let her find her way on her own, I had not yet made the connection to the similar beloofs that were still operating in my life. I had yet to learn that it is how we let ourselves crash, discover our subconscious beloofs that bring us to the crash, and then pick ourselves up and grow from each learning. It is each learning that makes the crashes less devastating and the learnings more enlightening.

So I return to cruising altitude. I now have two patents for hypnosis methods and devices, and win not just one, but two National Institutes of Health grants to study my technology with pregnant women to help them stop smoking. I close my private practice, and start flying high as a research scientist and technology developer. As I said, it is the 1990s in Seattle Washington, home to Boeing, Microsoft, Adobe, Costco, Amazon, Starbucks, and Sonicare, and musicians like Heart, Quincy Jones, Jimi Hendrix, and Kurt Cobain. My young ego beloof says I must compete, and to be "successful" must achieve similar success.

So I bring in a Microsoft millionaire as an investor in my business. It's just what you do—find an "angel investor" to provide the money necessary to get your startup off the ground. While he seems nice enough, I don't know that I'm climbing into a shark tank without knowing how to swim. He puts more and more money into the business and my young ego feels grateful that he "believes" in me the way he does. I would soon find out that his "belief in me" is my beloof.

I would learn after my fall, that my "partner" was one of the "sharks" Bill Gates and Steve Ballmer brought in to help them scavenge small technology companies to grow Microsoft after they squeezed Paul Allen out of the company. My investor had accumulated so much wealth from the early days at Microsoft that he belooved he had become a Bill Gates in his own right. And at the same time, I had become a tasty morsel—just the kind sharks like to feed on.

I believe my investor's intention had always been to acquire my company and my technology by squeezing me out. My only solace was that within three years of calling me into his office, telling me to pack up and be out by 4:00 PM that day, taking over my stock and the final year of my two-year grant, he had closed my business and lost his entire fortune. At the time, however, I was in shock and devastated. It would take me another five years of my own healing work for me to learn that he could steal my business, my grants, and my technology, but not my soul.

I spent those three years in shock, scrambling to provide income for my family and trying to keep my broken ego intact. I experienced two more failed business partnerships, followed by a complete emotional, spiritual, and psychic collapse. The shame of leaving my psychotherapy practice and failing at my attempts at business devastated any thoughts I might have about returning to my first profession. My battered ego piloted my Lear Jet directly into the side of a mountain.

I felt completely shattered and suicidally depressed. Ultimately, losing my business and all of my worldly possessions would be precisely the circumstances of the universe guiding me to identify and move on from the shadows of my primary beloofs. With the break I would begin to become conscious of, and fully experience, the vast expansiveness of my soul. The universe was leading me back to what I would later lovingly refer to as the Mother Ship—the Wellness Institute, for my own personal healing and recovery.

My beloved Mary Anne heard a message from the ethers that it was time for her to provide a keel for our rudderless ship. She took a job as a Geriatric Social Worker, and then a Mental Health Therapist in a clinic for indigent patients. For the next eight years she would take the lead in providing the financial stability we needed to survive while I resurrected my soul. I would spend the next year taking walks in the park with her and our Australian Shepard, Jake. We walked, and we talked, and we walked, and I breathed, and I rested, and I recovered. That year away from work would prove crucial for me to be present for my next learning.

The whole time Jessica and I were casting our big shadows, my younger daughter Liz was trying to find her way. She was overwhelmed in a fog of depression that was rolling in and engulfing her. With Jessica's ego and my ego doing battle, I wasn't able to attend to the needs Liz couldn't express, and she slowly developed a tendency to simply disconnect from what was going on. Her intelligence and perfectionism made her into the type of child I expected Jessica to be, and the type

Mary Anne was as a child; she carried a 3.9 cumulative average out of high school where she was on the varsity tennis team and homecoming court. So my beloof system was pleased with what appeared to be her "proper" development, and I assumed she was doing great!

What developed underneath that fog was a volcano of pressure growing up in an advantaged suburban community with friends who had outrageous amounts of disposable income while our family struggled to keep up with the level of wealth we were encountering around us; 16 year olds with a brand new Mercedes to drive and Visa and Nordstrom charge cards in their pockets were the norm. Alcohol and pot in the home also was the norm. While our family already encountered the carnage that alcohol and drugs can mete out and had a beginning knowledge of a family's recovery, we were like salmon struggling upstream to return to their spawning grounds. Liz was a time bomb, and deep in my subconscious I knew it.

Liz's crash first came at age 18, eight weeks into her career at the University of Southern California after winning a practically full-ride scholarship to study there. The call came one night from the emergency room at Cedars-Sinai Hospital. She had been brought there in a delusional state and was scared to death. We were devastated, although deep inside I was glad the volcano had finally erupted. I jumped on the next plane to Los Angeles, packed up my little girl, and brought her home. She was not herself and was struggling with her fragile grip on reality.

Since those devastating days in California, Liz's deeply spiritual soul has taught me more about the frailty of the human psyche than any psychology course or professional seminar I've taken. The mind was never intended to perform what we expect it to perform. And when our life experiences split us from our soul, we lose our rudder. We must step back and treat our beloofs and heal our trauma if we are to function as a complete "being." If we have not been provided with tools to maintain ourselves physically, psychically, emotionally, and spiritually, we are all just one step away from "insanity." We must first be informed that those tools exist and can be learned.

Liz moved back to our home in Seattle, took a term off, then attended Community College and returned to her old academic ways, graduating with high grades and entrance into the honor society. She transferred following graduation to Seattle University, moved into an apartment with a college friend and finished out her undergraduate degree magna cum laude, winning the top academic honor in the Sociology department. Just after her graduation ceremonies concluded, we all went out for Chinese food, and she joked that she had no idea where she would go from there. We all laughed, but I had the same sinking feeling I had when we left her at USC in Los Angeles.

Liz moved home following graduation, ostensibly to save up for a European trip she wanted to take before deciding her next step. She was hanging out with her old high school crowd, partying and drinking. A few weeks before her trip to Europe I found her outside the house in the middle of the night in a completely delusional state. I went directly into sympathetic shock and into action. It's our beloofs and our shadow parts that both serve us and dis-serve us. I drove Liz to the hospital and she was admitted to the psych ward a few hours later.

*"We admitted we were powerless and our lives had become unmanageable."*

I cried myself to sleep each night Liz was in the hospital just as I had each night Jessica was in Montana. *"God, grant me the serenity to accept the things I cannot change, the courage to change the things I can, and the wisdom to know the difference."* The difference these days was I could let myself feel, and I could let others comfort me.

I hate how we treat people in our "psychiatric" hospitals. We over-medicate people and provide little or no insight therapy or trauma healing. It would take two more hospitalizations before Liz would understand that while her friends might be able to party and drink, she could not. She was carrying so much shame about being "different" that my heart broke in half. The fixer in me could not fix this, even though I continued to try. I would tell her, "Think of it like diabetes; you have to take care of yourself in ways that others don't." What a lame piece of advice, but I had nothing else. How could she treat it like a common medical problem? My God, Mary Anne and I had devoted our professional life to mental health and there was no "cure" I could offer her. This was her Karma to learn about, along with learning how to heal. I felt my powerlessness and knew there was nothing I could do to help, other than love her and stay connected to her.

In Al-Anon they told me about the three C's: "You didn't create it, can't control it, and can't cure it." I learned to be grateful to Great Spirit for every part of her and every moment I spend with her. In the process, I learned to be grateful for every part of me also.

# 18

# Back to the Mother Ship

They say there are no coincidences. After selling our family home in 2003 we were able to live in a nice rental house just south of the city I found through an old friend. We're blessed with a beautiful view of Lake Washington and Mount Rainier and a monthly payment less than half of the bloated mortgage payment we created from pulling all the equity out of our Mercer Island house to cover our expenses with no income. I continued to be unemployed, something that hadn't happened since I was 11 and working my first newspaper route. My beloof system loathed not supporting oneself—it was unthinkable. But my ego is healing.

One day I went out to the mailbox and found tucked in between the morass of advertising circulars and junk mail a plain pre-printed 3x5 postcard. It was an invitation from the Wellness Institute for Mary Anne and me to attend an introductory gathering for people interested in becoming Certified Hypnotherapists and meeting with graduates of the program. We had graduated almost eight years earlier and we had no idea how they could possibly have found us since our address had changed. I looked at the invitation and said to Mary Anne, "Free food!"

There is an old Yiddish term: *Beshert*. The literal translation is "destiny." So if you hear an old Jew say the words, "It's *Beshert*," it means "it's destiny." Although we did not understand it at the time, the postcard from Wellness was *Beshert*.

When we walked into the dinner, Diane gave me a big hug and asked where we had been. She hadn't heard anything about me and had no idea of the trouble I had created for myself. The pain in Diane's face as I explained what had occurred during my absence was visible.

During my eight-year absence, Diane and David had created a two-year Internship Program for graduates of their six-day training: four long five-day weekends over a two-year span, about three months apart. After hearing my tale Diane said, "A new Internship is starting tomorrow. You must go home, pack a bag, and be back here at 7:00 AM sharp." I explained I had a full schedule the next two days and certainly did not have the tuition and room and board fees to pay. Again, she said in her own knowing way, a bit stronger this time, "You must go home, pack a bag, and be back here tomorrow. Everything else will work itself out if you simply show up." I turned to Mary Anne, who had stuck by me through the chaos and turmoil of the last few years, and she simply shook her head knowingly up and down.

I had stood with her throughout the tumult of her mid-20s when her mother died in open heart surgery at 67, and her father passed just eight months later at 83 of his broken heart. She bravely fought a deep depression that followed their loss, along with the loss of four other elders of her family the following year. She was my mate, and I would not let her down. I had never tested our relationship is a similar fashion— by falling apart. I believed I was ultimately strong and could weather any test. I would always be there for Mary Anne, and never need her to support me through my own crisis of being. When she looked at me and knowingly shook her head, I had to trust her judgment because mine had cracked in two. She gave me a hug, turned to Diane, and said, "He'll be there." I could not stop crying.

I never say that anything "saved my life"—that cliché just sounds so trite. Perhaps a better way to put it is that my experience at Wellness was truly "life changing." After completing my two-year Internship certification, I would complete the Personal Transformation Intensive leadership training. I also had never used the term "transformational" because I had never felt it myself. My experiences at Wellness were truly life changing and transformational.

Soon I began seeing a few clients again in the downstairs office of our rental house. When we rented it, I noticed it had a room in the basement with a private entrance. I introduced Heart-Centered Hypnotherapy into my work with clients and started seeing results I had never seen before. It made perfect sense, and clients both felt and understood the results on a cellular level. In the process of healing my personal beloofs, I was able to assist healing my client's beloofs, and it was easy. I was learning to channel universal energy rather than use my own personal energy in helping people to heal. I was releasing my "ego" therapist and connecting with my "soul" therapist. It would lead me ultimately to find my authentic self.

During our five-day retreat weekends at Wellness, no matter what level of certification or post-graduate work we are taking, we can participate in a morning spiritual practice of chanting followed by guided meditation. It is not a requirement to chant, but most of us have some degree of spiritual or religious trauma and it is a wonderful way to heal that trauma and perhaps create a clean, new spiritual connection.

Our teacher Diane spent a couple of years in a Hindu Ashram back in the 1970s on a spiritual journey while we laughed at the "Hari Krishnas" that hung out at the airport singing and dancing. We laughed at their Hindu garb and haircuts, and how they danced and sang seemingly without any self-consciousness. Diane is about six years older than me (about the same age as my oldest brother would be), so she began her spiritual journey before me. She had graduated in California with a Master's degree and spent a few years in social service agencies before being called to India. She came back to the U.S. transformed from the California girl who left, not knowing her path to having a clear vision of creating a healing place for therapists. I knew I needed healing, but for me, healing didn't need to include anything about God.

But then again, I was ready for anything that might help show me the way out my morass. The first time I sat down for chanting, I felt that I was being sacrilegious. Listening to the beautiful sounds of Krisha Das chanting "*Hari Krisha, Hari Rama, Rama Rama, Hari Hari,*" I actually felt it throughout my being and my body—that I was "wrong" to participate in a spiritual practice that was not said in Hebrew and included prayers to what could be seen as "false idols." But why would I feel "wrong"? More beloofs from the dualistic Judaism I had been taught? We were right, they were wrong? And the "they" was everyone who wasn't Jewish.

I encountered the same problem in reverse when confronted in college by Christian students who argued that if I did not accept Christ as the son of God—as a deity himself— I would not be allowed to enter the Kingdom of Heaven upon death. I laughed and replied, "Wow, now that's not a very Christian attitude." I knew full well that such dogma had never been a part of Jesus' teachings but was created by those who came after, and then really honed during the Middle

Ages. But here at Wellness, sitting in front of a beautiful altar listening to the spiritual tones that Krishna Das chants, I decide it really doesn't matter what I or others believe religiously because I am so far removed from any real connection or relationship with a higher power. All I know is that deep inside of me, I am frightened to death about the prospects of death.

So I decide to just sit and feel in a room brimming with spiritual energy, looking out over an altar of candles and beautiful religious objects listening to Krishna Das calling out his deep desire for spirit to hear, and to the response of those gathered with him, there and here and beyond. How can anyone calling out their desire for connection with the Universe, with the Mystery Beyond All Mysteries, with their Higher Power, be "wrong" in the method they choose?

We take time during open sharing to read and talk about the Hindu interpretation of its one God. It is important that we all take as much time as needed to talk about all of our experiences whatever they may be. It is an important part of our healing process. We learn that the deities described in the ancient Sanskrit Vedas of Hinduism simply represent all the wonderfully different aspects of the Hindu monotheistic God. As I begin to allow for the possibility that my beloofs are as right as everyone else, and as wrong as everyone else, I begin to re-examine my beloofs about the religion I was indoctrinated into along with the other religions I was exposed to. I discover that the real problem is my dualistic beloof system. Right vs wrong. Good vs bad. Success vs failure. Healthy vs unhealthy. My black and white world just does not fit for me anymore. I allow for paradox to enter my being. It is very uncomfortable for me to enter into a world of paradox.

*"We admitted we were powerless, that our lives had become unmanageable."*

*"God, grant me the serenity to accept the things I cannot change, the courage to change the things I can, and the wisdom to know the difference."*

I remember the night I left Liz at the hospital, crying my eyes out all the way home, and how repeating these two simple sentences brought me directly to peace and tranquility. The Mystery Beyond All Mysteries. And then one morning, while I am sitting in the temple room chanting with my Wellness buddies, tears begin to stream down my face. My mind says, "What's this?" and my heart says, "Shut up, fool." So I listen to my heart and my mind shuts up. My heart says, "You are connected to the Mystery. You'll survive." As natural tears begin to flow from my being, a glimmer of understanding that we are all "right" and we are all "wrong" when it comes to our beliefs emerges. At the same time that I sit with my tears chanting along with Krishna Das the ancient Sanskrit that I don't understand, not worrying about rightness or wrongness, I learn that my beloofs "feel." What a discovery. What a bitch.

Later that morning we are guided in a meditation by Yvonne, a senior Wellness teacher. Yvonne is simply the most beautiful spirit I have every encountered during my entire life. She is guiding us in a power spirit guide meditation. Guided meditation is wonderful. When I simply listen with my body rather than my mind and I surrender to the words that guide me, I enter into a euphoric state of relaxation and discovery that is indescribable.

Yvonne guides us into a very relaxed state, and then into a visualization of being on a beautiful path through a grassy meadow. I am approaching a wonderful fog up ahead. Yvonne says, "You realize that out of the fog will come a very important spirit guide for you. Allow this spirit guide to come to you in whatever form it takes; perhaps it is an animal, or an ancestor. Perhaps someone you recognize or not. Just let your spirit guide arrive in whatever form it takes."

Slowly, out of the fog of my meditation lumbers a wonderfully huge and ancient elephant. We come to stand nose to trunk.

Yvonne says, "You may ask your spirit guide any question you wish. Perhaps a decision you are trying to make, or the solution to problem you are having, or just some advice you need." Perfect! I know exactly what I'd like some practical advice deciding. Let's see if this spirit guide knows how to operate in the real world.

"OK, Great Spirit Guide, here we go: I'm trying to decide if we should stay in this wonderful rental house we have, or buy a new house while the market is coming down. I like the low rent and I don't have to do any work when something breaks or goes wrong, but I've owned a house since I was 27, and I like the pride of ownership. Also, I like the investment opportunity owning a house represents. It feels like when I rent, I'm throwing money away. But then again, I've really liked not having the responsibility of taking care of my own home. What should I do, oh great and mighty elephant?" I can feel the anxiety of the decision throughout my core.

After a time, the elephant looks deep into my soul with the infinite wisdom of the ages. His brown eyes are huge and compassionate and locked onto mine. He knows me better than I know myself. The elephant opens his mouth to speak and utters three unexpected and perfect words:

"What's a house?" he queries.

What's a house? I repeat to myself silently.

Oh my God, I immediately understand. The elephant never encounters such trivialities of the human mind. His "house" is wherever he lives at any given moment in time. "Renting" and "ownership" are not in his lexicon. The elephant lives a completely paradoxical life. He is knowledgeable of every universal truth and is aware that life is dichotomous at any given moment in time. He does not question birth, life, and death; he simply experiences them for what they are. Life is an ongoing mystery to the elephant from the moment he is born to the moment he dies. All his knowledge lies in his instincts. Could this work for me as a human being? All I have to do is release from each and every beloof I have adopted and learn to live instinctually again. Not a small task, and very scary to my tiny dualistic mind. I return from the fog and the grassy meadow completely enlightened about what a "home" really means to me.

At the end of the weekend, I rush home to tell Mary Anne about my discovery. I excitedly explain about the meditation and explain in great detail my question to the elephant. I get to the end and ask Mary Anne to guess what answer the elephant gives me. Without taking a breath, Mary Anne quickly says, "What's a house?"

I stumble back a couple of steps and almost fall over. "How did you know that?" I croak. She whispers, "I don't know."

I've come to believe in the collective unconscious—an energy that connects every molecule and every atom of everything in the universe. That's how déjà vu works. Mary Anne simply unconsciously experienced my meditation (and my spirit guide) along with me. Now I try to carry my elephant with me always and consult with him before making any decisions.

Since Mary Anne and I are humans and not elephants, and we like having a nice home to live in, we decided to look at houses to buy and trust that if one struck our fancy and we could put together a deal in a relaxed and joyous fashion, we would let the universe be our guide. About a year later we found an affordable new townhome near downtown Seattle, four blocks from a new light rail station they were building. Just six months after we bought our new home, the owner of the house we had been renting sold the property and we would have had to move anyway. *Beshert.*

# 19

# Soul Practice

I am reaching the end of my second year of Internship at Wellness and I have integrated Heart-Centered Hypnotherapy into my work with my clients. I am seeing great results. I now understand why I left my practice in the mid-nineties. I was burned out, feeling ineffective, and not doing my own work. I didn't know what I didn't know—that by leaving the Mother Ship I had separated from myself and from the collective unconscious, just as my beloofs had required.

But now, in the midst of my own recovery and reconnecting with my soul, my work as a therapist is transforming. The work energizes me and brings me joy. I am light and relaxed. I have integrated that my purpose is not what I do; it is who I am. My purpose is to show up in every moment of my life fully present and conscious, and to love my self and others unconditionally. Purpose is not a job, or the work I do, or the roles I play, or my client's experience. Purpose is my state of being.

My connection to my spirit guides grows stronger, and they inform my work with my clients. More of them start showing up in my life when I am present and conscious. I feel I am channeling the words that come from my mouth from an energy source that is infinite and all knowing. I am becoming the usher David spoke about, with the flashlight guiding people to their seats. Even now, as I write these words, I feel humble and self-conscious as my old beloofs try to rise up in me:

"Really?"

"Are you serious?"

"Spirit guides?"

"Channeling?"

"Who do you think you are? You've finally slipped over the edge into woo-woo-ville. You were taught that reality is based in observable evidence. What happened to the scientist in you? Have you considered this Wellness place is a cult and you've been brainwashed? Have you considered that you have finally gone mad?"

Actually, those are precisely the beloofs that kept me away from my own recovery for almost eight years and sent my Lear Jet crashing into the mountain. Again, you may judge what I just described as clinically absurd, psychotic, weird, woo-woo, transformative, amazing, or impossible. You may decide what I am saying is fact or fiction, or is real or unreal. You may believe that what I am experiencing is possible or impossible, or the ramblings of someone who should be taking anti-psychotic medication. It really doesn't matter to me. It is simply my experience, and what others think of me is none of my business.

In truth, there is something comforting when my old dualistic beloofs start to rise up in my consciousness. They help me discern and bring me back to paradox. Of course Wellness is a cult, as is Judaism, Christianity, Hinduism, Buddhism, and Nazism. Cult is not a dirty word: it is derived from the word "Culture."

Here is the definition of Cult:

*: a small religious group that is not part of a larger and more accepted religion and that has beliefs regarded by many people as extreme or dangerous*

*: a situation in which people admire and care about something or someone very much or too much*

*: a small group of very devoted supporters or fans*

Here is the definition of Paradox:

*: a statement or proposition that, despite sound (or apparently sound) reasoning from acceptable premises, leads to a conclusion that seems senseless, logically unacceptable, or self-contradictory.*

*: a seemingly absurd or self-contradictory statement or proposition that when investigated or explained may prove to be well founded or true.*

*"In a paradox, he has discovered that stepping back from his job has increased the rewards he gleans from it."*

Paradox: A cult can be any one of, or all of, its definitions at the same time. The Wellness Institute simply teaches an approach to life and healing from the perspective of paradox. Allowing competing beliefs and beloofs to exist as truth simultaneously has brought me a level of relaxation I had not imagined. When there is no "truth," I can both believe and disbelieve at the same time. I can be both right and wrong in the same instant. Pretty cool!

But for now, back to my story.

My practice is rebirthing in a way that I could not have imagined. I am re-energized and experiencing a joy in my life that was not possible since being born into such shock, grief, and fear. I complete my two-year Internship and take a year off before deciding to enroll in the next certification training, the Personal Transformation Intensive Leadership Training.

PTI Leaders are a small band of highly skilled trauma recovery therapists trained to lead five three-day weekend intensive retreats spread over five months, one weekend per month. There are three levels available in succession known as PTI One, PTI Two, and PTI Three. PTI One heals trauma. PTI Two creates change. PTI Three is known as "The Hero's Journey." The "three" series is a way for our clients to experience what we experience in the weekends we spend at Wellness. While David and Diane's main agenda was to heal the healers, along the way we decided why not our clients too. So we brought the same processes to the public.

I started doing PTIs with another colleague while Mary Anne decided to complete her two-year Internship and PTI Leadership training. While it was extremely satisfying to do PTIs with my Wellness colleague, it has been deeply moving to do PTIs with my spouse. David and Diane founded the Wellness Institute as a married couple and are deeply connected to each other as spouses, business partners, and soul mates. I believe it is their deep love and devotion to each other that has been the cornerstone of the processes and teachings they have developed throughout the years. Perhaps they did not even realize that the PTI courses are innately designed for couples to lead. While there are many PTI teams around the world doing amazing work, those of us who have the opportunity to conduct PTIs as couples are especially blessed. We are currently mentoring a married couple who are becoming PTI Leaders to take over for us as we retire from practice.

We have grown our PTI community as David and Diane have grown the Wellness community. Our graduates are connected in a way that people don't often have an opportunity to connect. By doing the same deep trauma recovery work that we do at Wellness, our clients have an opportunity to reconnect spiritually and in the collective unconscious. There is a palpable difference when we all gather, kind of like a non-denominational church on steroids. It's indescribable.

In my PTI Leadership Training program, we continue to work on our own issues using psychodrama in trance and energetic breath work. We are working on healing the very darkest parts of our psyche. In this venue, I find my work is far from over, and is definitely going deeper. I'm going back to the mat to start healing my shadow parts.

# 20

# Only the Shadow Knows

"Everyone carries a shadow," Jung wrote, "and the less it is embodied in the individual's conscious life, the blacker and denser it is." Jung also believed that "in spite of its function as a reservoir for human darkness—or perhaps because of this—the shadow is the seat of creativity." So theoretically, our shadows arise from the deepest, darkest side of our being to protect us from perceived harm. It both serves us, and dis-serves us concurrently. It is our dark side and our creative side at the same time; it is the epitome of paradox. Great! But by becoming intimately and consciously aware of our shadow parts, we can release the dark side, and engage the creative side from our higher self. Sound familiar? Star Wars, maybe?

Whenever I ask David which of Jung's volumes I should read, he always responds, "Don't! Jung is to be used as a reference, not studied linearly. He can make you crazy."

Just writing about this is starting to give me a headache, so back to my story.

For me to understand my own life, I've always turned to the "KISS" principle: "keep it simple, stupid!" Psychodrama in trance brings my shadows to my consciousness because they appear without warning. When I can actually experience them in action, and with the help of my cast and director, I can release from the parts that don't serve me and put the creative parts of those shadows to work for my higher good. Cool.

So here I am standing straight up in hypnotic trance with my psychodrama group gathered around me. I have regressed back to the situation with my business partner who "stole" my business. The "scene" is the day he called me into our conference room without warning. Seated there is a lawyer he hired as our "corporate attorney," a sleazy "partner" he hired on his own as a "marketing consultant" and a seat for myself. I sensed what was happening walking down the hall on the way into the conference room. For the psychodrama, I have selected individuals from my group to play each part and provided their lines for them.

"We've decided to separate you from the company," the actor playing my partner begins. Immediately I am back in that room experiencing everything I experienced that day. My stomach is turning flip-flops and I am going into deep shock. The fear is overwhelming. "What the hell have I done to myself?" my mind races.

Through my closed eyes, I look over to see the consultant sweating profusely and taking notes feverishly. His surrogate says, "Yes, separate you from the company so we can have it all to ourselves." He did not say those words in the real situation; in the actual meeting he was quiet throughout. However, in psychodrama we ask the players to say the lines that actually occurred and more importantly, the lines the characters were probably thinking but never said out loud.

The lawyer looks down at his notes. His line to himself, now said out loud in my psychodrama is, "This is going just as I planned. This Microsoft dude has plenty of money to pay for his little takeover. Ethics? What are ethics? This is just business. Don't take it personally, Rob."

The surrogate playing my ex-partner looks just past me at the wall behind. "I'm not firing you, Rob. I told you I would never fire you. We are just separating you for the good of the company." As I stand there listening to the psychodrama unfold around me, my subconscious reminds me that I knew this was coming since the day we first met. It was *Beshert*. It was my Karma, my silver platter, my teacher. "Fuck Karma!" my cognitive brain interjects. But the psychodrama is not to be denied.

"We appreciate all your service to the company, but we have decided to take it in another direction," my surrogate partner continues. As I see his face in front of my closed eyes, his eyes reflect a deep and dark shadow. I sensed its existence before, but now in psychodrama, it bursts forth in all its evil glory. Back in the actual situation, I boiled inside with anger, betrayal, and fear, but on that day these feelings did not come out into the light of day. On that day, I sat in that conference room, listened to his prepared speech, got up quietly, returned to my office, packed up my personal belongings from my office, walked to my car, and drove away in shock. I stood in my psychodrama circle in that same shock.

David begins tapping on my forehead. "Back to the source," he whispers. "Take yourself back to the source. A time, or place, or people that are the very source of these feelings."

I'm in my brother Michael's apartment shortly after his wife divorced him. The rest of my family is there also. He is rolling joints to take to the funeral, or wedding, or bar/bat mitzvah we're all going to. He carefully rolls each joint and places it in between the cigarettes in his pack of Winston cigarettes. My mother, father, and brother Alan watch almost in trance as the scene plays out. They are talking about the weather and other inane subjects. My mind is shrieking.

"Look at what he is doing!" I scream out silently. "Those are pot joints he is rolling. When you're not looking, he sneaks out behind the building and smokes them. Sometimes I go with him, or we go with some of our cousins. But he has lost his marriage and is failing at his business. He has no friends and has pushed away most of his family. He has a serious problem and we are standing around like everything is normal."

"Do something!" I shout inwardly. "Say something!" is what I wish I could say. And yet there I stand, silent, in shock.

David is standing with his face just a few inches from mine. It is so quiet I hear him breathing. I am standing in the middle of my group with all of this exploding in my head, showing no sign of anything. They have no idea because I am standing straight up as if nothing is wrong, but I am a ticking time bomb about to go off.

Suddenly and without forewarning, I am screaming out loud at David, at everyone, the words I never said in either event. I feel him jump back a few feet.

"Fuck you!! Fuck all of you!!!" I scream in a voice I have never heard out loud before. "You can all die for all I care. You don't care about me. You use me, take advantage of me, and blame me! FUCK YOU ALL! FUCK ALL OF YOU AND DIE!!!"

I drop to my knees in tears. I am sobbing uncontrollably. I am shaking like a leaf. I want to die. I have lost it. Years of rage with my brother and then with my business partner can no longer be contained. I am showing in public what I have never shown and promised myself never to show.

David's voice is back in my ear as I sit on the floor. He gently wants to help me put all this in a context I can use, even though I am still deep in trance. We are at a level in our work where we don't have to suffer in our past trauma. We have entered the realm of shadow work that allows us to change the effects of the trauma on a cellular level and move through the suffering to new ways of operating in our lives that work.

"What would you call these shadows; first the one that stays quiet, stuffs his feelings, and keeps the family secret?"

"The Caretaker," I say through my tears. Even before I was born I was elected to take care of my mother in the absence of my father, and then my older brother Michael since he was "sick."

"And this other one, the one that just appeared here in your psychodrama?" David suggests.

"You mean that angry one? That's not a shadow, that's how I really feel. Angry and betrayed," I jab.

"Are you sure it's not a shadow? He wanted to kill someone." David queried.

And then it all became clear. In one microsecond, it downloaded from the ethers for me to see and integrate.

If I had been clear and decisive about my feelings in the first place, when I first met this guy and sensed that he would betray me, I would never have brought this individual into my life. I knew deep in my soul he was dangerous and ill-intended from the moment I met him. But I thought I needed his money, so I sold out on my own feelings and integrity. I was bound to be betrayed and bound to be used. So my Caretaker went into action.

Of course my Caretaker was already fully trained and engaged as it had been in my family of origin with my mother and brother. In my current life, my caretaker found a new home with my wife and children. It was my job to support and take care of them no matter what. I mean, jeez, I did promise Mary Anne's dad I would.

And as I saw clearly in that nano-second of discovery, the shadow of my Tyrant was fully engaged also, just as my mother's had been. Throughout the early days of our marriage, I yelled and criticized Mary Anne, and when Jessica started going to school and showed signs of independence, I raged at her when she was not performing as I expected. At the time, I called it "righteous" anger; anger that I had a right to because someone else was not acting as I expected. But "righteous anger" was a beloof based on the teachings of my family of origin. In the Wellness model, I had adopted the victim position so I had to blame someone.

Jung said it this way: "A gentle and reasonable being can be transformed into a maniac or a savage beast. One is always inclined to lay the blame on external circumstances, but nothing could explode in us if it had not been there."

While I'm embarrassed to admit to these shadow parts, it helps to "come clean," as one of my clients calls it. I continue to make amends to everyone I exposed to my Caretaker and my Tyrant. In the 12 Steps of AA, it's called making "living amends," by apologizing for, and correcting, the offending behavior.

We always conclude a psychodrama with a new conclusion to replace the old beloof, and new decision to replace the old behavior. My old beloof was that when I felt unsafe, or felt I was about to be betrayed, my intuition must be faulty and must be questioned—I must be "wrong." My old decision was to countermand my intuition and plow ahead. I had to suck it up and take it all the way to the bitter end, no matter what my guts were saying. Hmmm…sounds familiar.

My new conclusion is that my intuition, my inner knowing, is always "correct" because it belongs to me and no one else. It is the paradox of being both right and wrong concurrently. To wonder if my intuition is either correct or incorrect is part of my dualistic beloof system. In a paradoxical world, both are true at the same time.

David came up to me after my psychodrama was over when I was out of trance and my eyes were open. He said, "Thank you for showing us your deepest shadow parts. It tells me how safe you feel doing your work here. Now you can make new and important decisions about how you treat the ones you love the most. Now you can discern when your shadows are driving the bus and when your authentic self is in charge."

I didn't quite know what he was talking about then—I was still integrating on a cellular level. Also, although I didn't know it at the time, I hadn't explored my Tyrant shadow deeply enough to release the part that did not serve me. But I became aware that a visceral shift was occurring at a very deep level. I came to understand later that the shift influences generations backwards and generations forward. When we make such changes at Jung's shadow level, we are helping heal those who came before us, and those who follow us.

In this single psychodrama, I learned how the shadow of my Caretaker fueled the shadow of my Tyrant. I learned that my shadows are layered and combine to form complexes; multiple shadows operating together both to protect me, and to make me vulnerable at the same time. What a paradox: beloofs and habits coexisting to both serve me and dis-serve me. I was overwhelmed, thinking I would never get to the "answer to all my problems" (dualistic beloof) and that I was "just a hopeless mess" (beloof). I work on those beloofs by choosing new beliefs and making them into mantras I repeat to myself.

"I am relaxed and comfortable"

"My spirit guides are with me and guide me"

"I heal my beloofs at a deeper and deeper level"

"I am exactly where I am supposed to be, and what is happening in my life is exactly what is supposed to be happening"

"I am that I am"

"I am that I am"

"I am"

Breathing into these new beliefs and decisions, I begin to stop ruminating about the past and worrying about the future. I actively meditate regularly on my new beliefs. When beloofs about the past or future intrude into my mantra, I gently turn up the volume of my new beliefs and decisions. There are many times I must turn up the volume to maximum to drown out the noise of my own monkey brain. Bit by bit, with daily work, my beloofs and the shadow behaviors they feed quiet and fade. I remember the reason Jung called them shadows is that while with consciousness they recede back into the dark part of my being, they still lurk there, ready to burst forth when my beloofs call out to them. I decide to diligently remain conscious of my shadows' earliest peek out of the darkness, remembering that they formed at a very young time in my life to protect my injured inner child, and I compassionately ask them to stand down while I call on my new conclusions and decisions to guide me from my highest self.

# 21
# Will I Ever Graduate?

It is September 11, 2001. Mary Anne and I were married on September 12, 1976. It is the day before our 25th wedding anniversary and we have reservations for the upcoming weekend at the Rosario Resort on Orcas Island, one of the San Juan Islands of Puget Sound. It is a beautiful old resort on a beautiful rural island.

It is Tuesday morning, and I am up early getting ready to jump on our treadmill for a morning workout. Since my TV addiction is serious, I turn it on to watch the morning news while I work out. The very first image I see is the World Trade Center burning. At first I think I've left the TV on a movie channel from the night before and I'm watching a spy movie. But then I see Aaron Brown's face trying to explain what is happening. I knew Aaron Brown from the years he reported the local news for the Seattle affiliate. We were all so proud he had made it to the national news on CNN. September 11, 2001 was his first day reporting.

As I start to understand that this is really happening before my eyes, I slowly slump into the overstuffed chair in the living room of our home. At some point, Mary Anne comes in and I bring her up to speed. We watch in horror and silence for the next hours.

We had both lived through the assassinations of John F. Kennedy, Robert Kennedy, Martin Luther King, Kent State, and the eight (official) years the United States participated in the Vietnam War. There were race riots in Dayton, Ohio in 1966, ostensibly started by the murder of a black bootlegger by white interlopers.

No one knows the real story, but Dayton was a powder keg of racial tension, and anything could have set it off. I was a 17-year-old sophomore at Wright State University living with my parents in racially diverse Dayton View. We watched out the front windows of our house on Lexington Avenue as Jeeps filled with National Guard troops patrolled the neighborhoods with live 50-caliber machine guns mounted on the back manned in readiness for anything. We could see the glow in the sky as the looters burned the African American businesses on Third Street. One of my parents' friends was shot and killed inside of his store trying to protect his inventory. I watched through my three-year-old's eyes still in shock from the Holocaust, and my six-year-old eyes standing in the back of our Synagogue sanctuary watching the film of the carnage of Auschwitz. They are the same eyes that saw the mangled bodies in the daily news pictures of the soldiers we sent to Vietnam, some of them my high school compatriots, and I felt nothing.

They were the same eyes that looked on when we heard news of John F. Kennedy's murder over the loudspeaker at our high school. The same eyes that saw Robert Kennedy dying on the floor of the hotel where he had spoken, and the same eyes that saw the picture of Martin Luther King lying dead on the balcony of his motel as his aides pointed skyward toward the source of the bullets.

Perhaps if I actually had felt my feelings in those days, I might have gone crazy or committed suicide. The shadow of shock served me well there. I continued to function well even through the suffering I did not know existed. Shock is what allowed Jews to come out of the concentration camps and return to some sort of life, albeit scarred. The shadow of shock serves us all at times of deep trauma and suffering—until it starts a life of its own called PTSD.

I felt my feelings just enough to be angry about the unjust war in Vietnam, just enough to stand up to my World War II father who believed that every war the United States entered into was just and necessary. He and I almost came to physical blows over Vietnam, until my mother finally found her voice and yelled, "He's right, Jack, he's right!"

I felt my feelings just enough to become an anti-war activist and a Vietnam War protester. I was prepared to go to Canada if necessary until a medical condition served to help me flunk my draft physical. The feelings that dwelled in my subconscious were my deep sense of sadness and grief, just under a thick layer of ancestral shame.

And so, watching 9-11 unfold before our eyes in live living color, as the twin towers collapse and disintegrate, my shock and horror kick in, thank God. Underneath, my well of repressed sadness, grief, and shame grows deeper.

Here are the CNN statistics from 9-11:

"At the World Trade Center site in Lower Manhattan, 2,753 people are killed when hijacked American Airlines Flight 11 and United Airlines Flight 175 are intentionally crashed into the north and south towers.

Of those who perish during the initial attacks and the subsequent collapses of the towers, 343 are New York City firefighters, another 23 are New York City police officers, and 37 others are officers at the Port Authority.

The victims range in age from two to 85 years. Approximately 75-80 percent of the victims are men.

At the Pentagon in Washington, 184 people are killed when hijacked American Airlines Flight 77 crashes into the building.

Near Shanksville, Pennsylvania, 40 passengers and crew members aboard United Airlines Flight 93 die when the plane crashes into a field. It is believed that the hijackers crashed the plane in that location, rather than their unknown target, after the passengers and crew attempted to retake control of the flight deck."

And now healing tears fill my eyes as I write these words nearly 15 years later.

May all their spirits rest in peace and their souls return purified and renewed.

Mary Anne and I decided to celebrate our 25th anniversary on Orcas Island on September 12, 2001. It was bitter and sweet at the same time. And we experienced shame about celebrating our first 25 years together in the shadow of trauma our country was experiencing.

Shame is such a tricky beloof. I think of it as guilt on steroids. Guilt is the feeling I feel when I do something I regret. It allows me to take responsibility and make changes. Shame is the beloof that something in me is deeply defective and cannot be fixed. I must hide it lest someone see it and discover my fraud. It is unchangeable and I am forever doomed to take these flaws to my grave. It is based in my ancestor's beloofs in their own shame, and the faulty thinking I created as a little one in times of trauma when I was unable to function "properly."

So until I shed my ancestral shame and the shame of the beloofs I collected long ago, I will continue to operate under the influence of the complex of shadows including my shock, Caretaker, and Tyrant to keep my shame secret. And the way to release myself of shame is to briefly revisit the origins of the beloof, feel my true emotions that the shame covers, and release those feelings consciously. With the release of shame and my ability to discern then from now, I can reframe the beloofs into new conclusions and decisions. Great! I get it! I'm good! Do I get to graduate now?

Mary Anne says, "When we draw our last breath."

Fuck!

# 22

# Joy

*"What's all this bullshit about being happy?*
*Life is not happy!"*
–Sylvia Levin Speigel, my mother

Now my practice is doing well, and my PTIs are filling up completely. I am so energized by doing my own work and seeing the same work bringing amazing transformations to my clients. I have more energy than I had twenty years earlier, and we are recovering from our financial collapse. Mary Anne is completing her PTI training and we are starting to plan to be in practice together again since our children have reached young adulthood.

I am at Wellness, now participating in our "Mentors" program. All of us in Mentors have completed our two-year Internship and one-year PTI Leadership Training Certifications. We are becoming the "elders" of Wellness, hence the term "Mentors." If we are leading PTIs, we are considered teachers.

I am sitting in the circle feeling relaxed and well cared for during a simple share—nothing serious going on here, no heavy, deep, and real process that is triggering me. Suddenly, I begin to feel a rolling sensation in my gut. It really catches my attention. I wonder about the foods I've eaten earlier and write it off as a bit of indigestion. However, the rolling sensation is increasing in intensity and I begin to have a panicky feeling. I'm about 58 years old, and in denial that 60 is right around the corner. I start thinking about heart attacks and ambulances. The rolling intensifies. It is feeling like a Tsunami, coming in deep waves of energy. Being true to my beloofs, I say nothing and try to appear "normal."

A break comes, and the rolling is now scaring me. I approach both David and Diane, and they have me describe the sensations in detail. I tell them what I am experiencing and they listen intently. They are very careful about medical emergencies, and I tell them that maybe I should drive myself up the road and get checked out at the emergency room. "I mean, it really feels like there is something physically wrong with me," I plead.

They suggest I sit with the feelings and see if they resolve overnight. Diane makes one more suggestion: "Let the feelings have a voice and see what they have to say to you. Ask them why they are here and what they represent." I think to myself, "Jeez, Diane, can you get any more woo-woo here? I could be dying here and you suggest I have a conversation with my body. Jeez Louise!"

So I have my dinner and hang out with my Wellness buddies. They support me going up to the emergency room to get it checked out if that's what I need to do. I go to bed and try to relax into the rolling waves going on in my entire gut. They get stronger. So I take Diane's crazy approach.

"Hello rolling sensation in my gut; how are you doing?" No response. My body knows I'm just screwing around and won't cooperate. The rolling gets worse.

"OK, I'm serious now. You are scaring me. Who are you, and why are you here?"

The response comes back clear and concise. "I am your joy. You lost track of me when you came here."

"My joy?" I respond. "My joy...? I feel joy, don't I?"

I laugh and screw around all the time. I have a great repertoire of jokes for all occasions. I've ridden motorcycles and I'm a scuba diver; I've hiked the Grand Canyon and camped in most of the National Parks; I've taken my kids to Hawaii and vacationed all over the country. We visited both Disney parks and rode all the rides (not admitting how scared I was). I've gone to plays, and concerts, and played musical instruments and practiced the arts. I've experienced joy, haven't I?

Lying here in the darkness of the dormitory room of the Wellness Institute, the rolling in my gut increases and I feel a deep grief come over me. The grief envelops me and is not to be denied. How can one go through their entire life without the experience of true joy? It devastates me.

"I am your joy," I hear loud and clear. "You've been so frightened for so long, you lost track of me. You can have me back if you like."

The rolling does not subside, but my fear of it abates a bit.

"Joy: noun

: *a feeling of great pleasure and happiness*"

A FEELING of great pleasure and happiness.

So while I've been having all these wonderful experiences in my life, I forgot how to feel real joy. In fact, it went with the shock and loss of most of my emotions.

Remember the look in the eyes of my three year old? His eyes are vacant of emotion. The loss of John, Robert, and Martin—I didn't feel it, did I. The joy of doing my own Bar Mitzvah so well and everyone being so proud of me? Nope. The joy of my wedding to Mary Anne? Too

much alcohol and pot. The joy of coming eyeball to eyeball with Jessica just seconds after her birth? I don't think so. The joy of watching Liz dance in her tutu on stage at four years old? Not even a bit.

Could it be that all this work I've been doing—the hypnotherapies, the psychodramas, the breath work, examining my shadows, managing my energy and my addictions—could it be just the glimmer of a chance that my joy is re-emerging? Recalling that time I had with my creator in the inter-life, my Mystery beyond all Mysteries, when the voice quietly said to me, "Teach Peace, Teach Peace," there was no fear. I was safe. I learned that I was not alone in this body and never have been.

So how did the fear return? Not with the time I spent in the Civil War—I sensed it was later, not yet revealed. So I put a bookmark in place to explore that later. For now, I want to experience the return of the joy rolling through my guts like a train.

Now the tears come flooding again.

But not tears of pain: tears of joy.

And the rolling in my gut turns into rolls of laughter.

My dorm mates have no idea of what's going on with me, laughing and crying at the same time. They probably think I've finally slipped over the edge but I really don't much care. It's just how we roll.

The next day David and Diane pull me aside to see how I'm doing. I tell them the whole story of the night before and they both begin to laugh. "We knew it was Kundalini energy, but you had to find out for yourself. It's very common when people do this work that they experience the return of their Kundalini energy, and it can feel quite overwhelming at first until you understand it."

I curse them silently and say, "Then why didn't you just tell me?" David replied, "Knowing you, you would not have believed us anyway. You had to find out for yourself." They know me far too well.

Kundalini: (From Wikipedia)

"Kundalini (Sanskrit kuṇḍalinī, कुण्डलिनी, 'coiled one'), in yogic theory, is a primal energy, or Shakti, located at the base of the spine. Different spiritual traditions teach methods of 'awakening' kundalini for the purpose of reaching spiritual enlightenment. The Yoga Upanishads describe Kundalini as lying 'coiled' at the base of the spine, represented as either a goddess or sleeping serpent waiting to be awakened. In modern commentaries, Kundalini has been called an unconscious, instinctive, or libidinal force, or 'mother energy or intelligence of complete maturation.'"

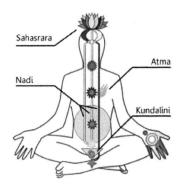

Kundalini awakening is said to result in deep meditation, enlightenment and bliss. This awakening involves the Kundalini physically moving up the central channel to reach within the Sahasrara Chakra at the top of the head. Many systems of yoga focus on the awakening of Kundalini through meditation, pranayama breathing, the practice of asana, and chanting of mantras."

What an amazing experience! But I am still haunted by that fear I bookmarked…

# 23

# The Holocaust Reprise

Why is it that whenever I think I will have a nice, relaxing, integrative breath work, there are always fireworks? Yes, a beloof. Get it?

The bookmark—right: that bookmark.

We bookmark our work, just like we bookmark a good book we are reading to remember something about where we left off. So last time I bookmarked my work was about how the fear returned. The amazing thing about having lots of experience doing breath work is that I can simply set an intention, and there is a great likelihood I will survive the experience with a bit more enlightenment. All it takes is, "I intend to discover the source of the fear I brought to this life or experienced in this life that blocked my Kundalini energy," and then rock and breathe. So that's what I do.

Quickly, I am back in the gas chamber. Fuck! Gasping, coughing, trying to move through the concrete blocks to the outside where there is fresh air. The concrete will not give, and again I am dying an agonizing death.

What more am I to learn by re-experiencing this horrible ending? What could I have missed the first time I re-lived this terrible death in this very same gas chamber? This awful, painful death. Again? Really?

I get it. I'm an egotistical rich guy. I have servants, and cars, and drivers, and fine art, and expensive china, and live in an opulent house, and live an opulent lifestyle. I don't see the looks of scorn and resentment from those I employed. They should be grateful for the life I "give" them, shouldn't they?

I'm so arrogant I don't see the danger that is happening right before my eyes. I represent what the Nazis hate. I'm a wealthy, successful Jew. I hadn't come into money; I made it all myself. Why would they resent my success; the same opportunities were there for them, weren't they? Why would they want to take from me what I lawfully earned? It isn't right. They would never do that, would they?

My wife felt, sensed, what was going on and left with the children. I decide my property is worth more to me than my family and my life. If I sacrifice all I worked for, I would cease to exist. I have no choice and they have no right. The world will never let genocide happen. I mean, it never happened before, had it?

My this-life cognitive brain interrupts; "How fucking naive can one past incarnation be?"

I am ashamed of him, but I understand how he could have tagged along into this life. But why am I going over this again? I've already been here. I explored the beloofs I carried with me from this past life and released them. I already muttered the words to detach from this poor lost spirit and send him to the light, but just to make sure, I utter them again:

"I hereby release any and all attachments and contracts I may have made with this spirit and release him to go to the light."

I breathe into my body fully expecting the residual fear I carried into this life to be released.

It is not.

So I breathe into the fear again and ask it to speak.

"Who are you?" I ask.

"The fear of the others," the fear replies quietly.

"What others?" I continue, the fear doubling.

"The others in the gas chamber who died in terror with me that day," comes the response.

"Holy God in Heaven," my sitter hears me gasp out loud, as I begin to actually feel the other souls who attached to my soul as we all died together that day. Not a few, not one hundred, but hundreds of souls are attached to me in that gas chamber as we gasp our final breaths together. Wisps of them are still attached to the spirit that occupies this body lying on the floor of the Wellness Institute. The number 800 comes to me from beyond.

I desperately whisper to my sitter, "Get Yvonne, now!" My lower back is on fire with pain.

Most of the time I experience Yvonne as not being of this planet. She herself says she's been here 3000 years, and might be moving on soon. The sly grin that spreads across her lips as she says it says she just playing with me, but most of me thinks not. She is a classically trained Ph.D. psychologist and one of the best mental health professionals I've ever met. But she is something so far beyond that. I hate the term "shaman" since it's been used by charlatans so much, so I just refer to people like Yvonne as Healers with a capital "H." It's a mystery how she works, and she just knows what to do. She refers to herself as an energy worker.

I feel Yvonne come over to my mat and hear her whisper, "What's going on?"

"He just asked for you. He's back in the gas chamber," my sitter quietly replies.

Yvonne brings her ear to my mouth and says, "What's going on, Rob?"

There is so much terror in my body I can hardly be heard.

"There are too many," I squeak.

"Too many what?" Yvonne asks.

I am shaking violently. "Too many souls…they're suffocating me with their fear. I'm trying to help them to the other side, but there are too many and I don't believe in the other side myself. Their terror is freezing me, and keeping me from passing over. I'm trying to take them with me but there are just too many. Help me—they are attached at my back."

I immediately feel Yvonne's hands and her energy at my back. My sitter has joined with her in her work. In Mentors we are all experienced with helping someone energetically release attachments from their bodies and their souls, so I know what is going on and I am helping them the best I can by visualizing the attachment energies releasing. They are pulling imaginary cords out of my lower back and cutting them free by snapping their fingers. When I first saw this happen, I thought I was watching snake oil salesmen at work: Louisiana Cajun Voodoo being practiced. But having both seen and experienced the release that happens on a visceral level, I know it to be a valid treatment mechanism—at least for me and most of the people we treat.

The pulling and snapping continues and I start to feel my terror and an incredible physical weight releasing from my lower back. They are working feverishly and I am letting them help me. I become conscious that I have been carrying these 800 souls throughout my life. I have carried their terror and their weight. None wanted to die that day, and they attached to me in a desperate attempt to hang on. In this moment, I become aware that these are the attachments that birthed the shadow of my overactive caretaker in this life and in the process blocked my pure experience of joy.

As Yvonne finishes her work with me, she is helping to move this poor spirit finally on to the other side. She says to me (him), "You can look up now into the beautiful purple white light that is coming down surrounding you in complete and forever lasting safety and protection. As the light surrounds you, you are lifted and cradled in the arms of your creator. You can go now; you are safe."

I am reminded of my time with my creator after the lifetime as the young Revolutionary War soldier. I know this spirit is going to the safety of the Great Mystery, and there is nothing to be afraid of ever again. I am guiding the 800 freed souls that attached to me into the light, and as their fear dissolves so does mine. It is their fear and not mine that I carried into this life.

And then the strangest and most powerful understanding of my entire lifetime comes to me. It is a pivotal shift in consciousness that forever changes me.

As my past life spirit enters the light of the collective, I look down from above upon the Holocaust. I look down and see Auschwitz, and Treblinka, and Buchenwald, and Hitler, and all the carnage that the Nazi's are bringing upon our world. I look down upon the bodies piled in neat rows in the mass graves, and the millions quietly lined up to meet the gas chambers we died in. I look down now through my Creator's eyes.

And I understand. I understand. And I cry, and I cry, and I cry.

Not tears of grief and loss, but tears of deep understanding that the universe is perfect in its construction even in a horrendous event like the Holocaust. I cry for the Jews and at the same time, I cry for the Nazis. I cry tears that I am not alone, and that the Mystery Beyond all Mysteries is at work at this very moment in time, and in all the different moments of my many lifetimes; and also in the all the moments of my death times.

I feel tremendous compassion for the Jews and others who meet the end of their life in the Holocaust, and especially for the family members left behind. And I feel tremendous compassion for the Nazis who murder them, and for the generations that follow them.

I know these words might cause great distress and anger for the reader who lives each day trapped in anger or grief or despair in the shadow of the Holocaust. I offer my deepest apology if that is the case for you. It is not my intent to minimize or ignore your personal experience and pain. When I stood at age five or six in silent shock on Yom Hashoah (Day of Remembrance) at the back of the sanctuary of my synagogue listening to the Rabbi shout in a loud and angry voice, "We will never forget what happened to us here, and we will remember always how God abandoned us," I felt the same anger and spiritual betrayal. But I was just a small child soaking up everything around me like a sponge. Without knowing it consciously, I became deeply fearful and alone in those words. They went so deep inside of me and created the beloofs that I am a victim and alone in the world to make my way; the beloof that God is non-existent or has abandoned me. A spiritual split was created that I would not be able to heal until this day and in this way.

Those beloofs birthed the shadow of the Orphan and the Tyrant, shadows in which I would invest much of my valuable energy and resources over the first portion of my life. Although not as frequently, I continue to hear those same words repeated by friends and religious leaders in some of the traditional readings of Jewish text, and they trouble me, especially when uttered in the presence of small children.

Some years ago one of my teachers, Ram Dass, wrote a letter to the parents of a twelve-year-old girl named Rachel who one seemingly normal day said goodbye to her parents, walked away to meet some friends, and was abducted and violently murdered. His words reflect this same visceral understanding I experienced that day on my breath work mat and bring me peace when I re-read his letter to them:

*Dear Steve and Anita,*

*Rachel finished her work on earth, and left the stage in a manner that leaves those of us left behind with a cry of agony in our hearts, as the fragile thread of our faith is dealt with so violently. Is anyone strong enough to stay conscious through such teaching as you are receiving? Probably very few. And even they would only have a whisper of equanimity and peace amidst the screaming trumpets of their rage, grief, horror and desolation.*

*I can't assuage your pain with any words, nor should I. For your pain is Rachel's legacy to you. Not that she or I would inflict such pain by choice, but there it is. And it must burn its purifying way to completion. For something in you dies when you bear the unbearable, and it is only in that dark night of the soul that you are prepared to see as God sees, and to love as God loves.*

*Now is the time to let your grief find expression. No false strength. Now is the time to sit quietly and speak to Rachel, and thank her for being with you these few years, and encourage her to go on with whatever her work is, knowing that you will grow in compassion and wisdom from this experience. In my heart, I know that you and she will meet again and again, and recognize the many ways in which you have known each other. And when you meet you will know, in a flash, what now it is not given to you to know: Why this had to be the way it was.*

*Our rational minds can never understand what has happened, but our hearts—if we can keep them open to God—will find their own intuitive way. Rachel came through you to do her work on earth, which includes her manner of death. Now her soul is free, and the love that you can share with her is invulnerable to the winds of changing time and space.*

*In that deep love, include me.*

*In love,*

*Ram Dass*

In that moment lying on my mat breathing, as my past life spirit along with the 800 others still attached to me in this life released to the light, I knew in a flash what then had not been given to me to know; why the Holocaust and every other trauma I experience in my life has to be the way it is. That my Creator is present in every experience of my life, including my death. That every person I travel with in this life is my teacher, even one that might harm me. That every event I experience represents the laboratory of my life.

I have the choice to experience my life dualistically or paradoxically; that is my personal opportunity, my own free will. I can judge my experiences to be good or bad, right or wrong, success or failure. Or I can instruct the dualistic judgments of my beloofs to stand down, and simply feel what I feel in everything I experience; at times deep sadness, other times exquisite grief; a flash of anger, sudden hurt, abounding joy—feeling with my whole body as my emotions remind me that I am alive and well.

In my work, I've had occasion to treat people whose ancestors were Nazis who actively participated in the Holocaust. The understanding of my past life exploration allows me to see past any anger and blame I might have experienced when I was younger. The scars of their heritage and the beloofs they carry are deep and abiding in their life. They carry the heavy shame of their ancestors. My compassion and empathy for them is deep. May we all continue to heal, and to learn, and to grow together in the collective.

Ram Dass experienced a devastating stroke at age 64. He accepted it as a teaching. He said, "But here I am, 'Mr. Spiritual', and in my own death, I didn't orient towards the spirit.

It shows me I have some work to do.

It shows me because that's the test. That's the test. So I flunked the test."

Ram Dass went on to recover as much as possible from his stroke, and finished his book, *Still Here*. He spoke about how God "stroked" him so he could deepen his spiritual connection further. I love Ram Das, and yet I have never been in his physical presence. He feels like a brother to me—that he knows me at the deepest level possible. His teachings have helped me to become a more loving and spiritual being. His presence in my life, even though we have never been in the same room together, is completely palpable to me. He is pure love, just like his teacher Maharaji. Someone once said of Maharaji, "What staggered me is not that he loved everybody, but that when I was sitting in front of him, I loved everybody."

I am still learning to emanate love from every cell of my body, unconditional love for myself, and unconditional love for everyone. I am learning to experience exquisite joy in this life. May the spirit of my past life brother rest in eternal peace along with the people who stole from him and murdered him, and may all their souls find exquisite joy and happiness in their new beginnings.

# 24

# Processing the Reprise

After a breath work session, we have lots of time to process the meaning of the session content into our consciousness so we can integrate the new conclusions and make new decisions on how we wish to operate in our lives and our relationships. That's the beautiful nature of doing work in retreat. The cognitive work is as important as the trance work for real transformation to happen in our lives. Otherwise, the work can slip away into the subconscious and the old beloofs may become operant again.

So after my session, I went to my teacher Yvonne and my sitter and asked to have a copy of their session notes and talk about their observations of my work. These are Yvonne's actual notes with my parenthetical editorial notes in italics. Be forewarned; while Yvonne considers herself a scientist she is highly metaphysical, so much of what she shares is theoretical. However, with the realness of my personal experiences, I've come to accept that what might sound wildly theoretical is no more or less believable than the beloofs I carry from other theorists.

*Session Notes*
Key points:
You had a past life/parallel life split …
> *(Metaphysics explains that time is a construct created by humans, and is not necessarily linear. The past is not necessarily behind us and the future is not necessarily in*

*front of us. What we beloove to be the future might just be the past and what we beloove to be the past might just be the future. In addition, we could be living in a parallel lifetime that is split off from us and unknown to us, or our two lifetimes might just overlap each other. Yvonne believes that my past life as the rich German man who died in the gas chamber, overlaps with my current life in this incarnation and exists in parallel. When I become conscious of this possibility, I can ask the past life shadow parts to stand down so I can live this life purely.)*

Holocaust: the Rich Man (Progressive and rebellious)

Arrogant, Entitled

Self-deceiving

Knows what is good for everyone

Refuses to become aware of how his family would be affected

Lost the connection with his soul

Died feeling lost, confused, and giving up (became compliant)

*(Just ask my wife and children if they think I know what's good for everyone. I battle this shadow everyday—I call him the Righteous Tyrant, and try to keep him in a strong cage under lock and key. I use the positive qualities of this shadow to help clients who come to me to learn, or when people ask for my opinion directly. See the words "became compliant"? That was the first 16 years of my life. What follows parallels my life up to age 50.)*

Current Life: The Immature Feminine (Regressive, abused self)

Weak

Slick

Manipulating

Helpless

Blind

Self-deceiving

Reckless

Lost

No connection with the soul

Feels worthless and a fraud

No Intuition activated

> *(These are the qualities of the parallel life with the rich man of the Holocaust. They represent a completely traumatized feminine side, hence her note 'Immature feminine'. The negative qualities she lists are the shadow parts of the injured feminine from my past life in the Holocaust. They operated in my life from my unconscious beloofs brought with me.)*

The Autonomous Complex: (The Head)

> *(An autonomous complex is a combination of shadow parts working together, kind of like an orchestra of learned traits creating a cacophony of chaos in our lives. The autonomous complex operates out of our head as a complex of behaviors based on our beloofs.)*

Controls everything and everybody

Has all the answers; does not listen to anyone

Makes all the decisions

It is the Motherboard, the Central Processing Unit

Runs all the systems in the essence

Prime director

Blind

Talks all the time

No intuition activated

Turns down the volume of the heart ... No feminine activated
No feeling
No real direction
Keeps everything in its place
Keeps everything separate.

> *(Not very pretty, and a bit overwhelming, but at least now I know. And here comes the best part!)*

Healing:
Being present with the merging of the soul and body
Integration into the heart
Using what is FELT rather than the words
Listening for the TRUTH of who you are
Using Intuition that comes from the Heart and the Soul
I am One. I am Whole. I am Connected

> *(The words in the last line are my own words, which I proclaimed at the end of my session. We always create our own new beliefs to replace our old beloofs before we end the session. These words were written on a 3x5 inch card and I say them to myself daily as a mantra of meditation.)*

I am One.
I am Whole.
I am Connected.
I Teach Peace.

# 25

# Why Hypnosis?

I guess it would be good to tell the story of how I got interested in hypnosis in the first place. I first described my experience in 1981 in an article I was asked to write for a small suburban newspaper when we opened our very first private practice. This is taken from that article:

The moments that have defined my destiny are crystal clear in my memory. Such is this one.

In the summer of 1960, as an 11-year-old boy, my oldest brother and his friend were participating in a study at Wright Patterson Air Force Base testing human factors for extended weightlessness. They were taught self-hypnosis and post-hypnotic suggestion as a mechanism to ameliorate physical stress and emotional fear. No one knew at that time that the United States planned to send a human being to the surface of the moon within the next 10 years.

For fun one warm Saturday afternoon, the two of them had me stretch out on a table in our garage, and asked me to relax and drift into a deep state of rest. I waited for the "hypnotic trance" to take effect, sending me into a blissful state of unconsciousness. Instead, while I did experience a very relaxed state, I remembered everything they said and my expected trip into "unconscious hypnotic trance" never happened. This was one of the many beloofs I held about hypnosis.

I got up from the table in the garage "knowing" that hypnosis did not work. They had given me post-hypnotic suggestions to wake up precisely at 3:00 AM, get out of my bed, put on my clothes, go out to our garage, take my bike out, get on, and ride one time counter-clockwise around our city block. Interesting that I remember their words verbatim to this very day 55 years later.

As instructed during the hypnosis, I awoke from my sleep precisely at 3:00 AM, wide awake. I had not set an alarm, and clearly saw the time on my clock when I awoke. I immediately realized I was in complete control of my actions and could choose to go back to sleep if I wished. Instead, I put on my clothes as I was asked to, walked calmly down the stairs and out the back door to that same garage, got out my trusted bike, jumped on, and in the darkness, took exactly one trip counter-clockwise around our city block. I was unaware that my brother and his friend were nervously observing from his bedroom above. I returned about 10 minutes later, put the bike away, climbed the stairs back to my bedroom, took off my clothes and fell quickly back to sleep. I awoke the next morning feeling great, and remembered everything I had done.

I was aware that I had performed precisely the suggestions they had made and consciously understood that I might have simply been trying to please my big brother and his friend. For whatever reason, I was compelled to do as they had suggested. Was I "hypnotized," or simply a little brother trying to please his big brother? I still cannot honestly answer that question. However the larger question that still haunts me to this very day and that I still seek to fully understand is what was it that awakened me to look at a clock on my nightstand that was pointed precisely at 3:00 AM?

Much later, in 1972, a man named John Wolf lectured a clinical practice class I attended at the University of Michigan graduate school. As we all pulled out our notebooks and pencils ready to try to stay awake through another boring lecture, he asked us to push back our chairs and lie flat on the floor. That never happened before. He instructed us in a precise fashion to alternately tense and relax certain muscles in our body. His voice was calm and soothing. After a few moments I was experiencing a level of relaxation I had never known. At one point I heard him say something about floating and felt my body lose contact with the floor. My conscious mind knew that gravity still worked, I just didn't care to acknowledge it. After a time, I heard him say "3, 2, 1, eyes open and wide awake," and I was back in the room. I felt great! He asked us to estimate how much time had elapsed, and I figured about 10 minutes. We had been lying there for over 30. He then taught us about "autogenic" training—using relaxation training, visualization, and guided imagery for self-directed healing. The skeptic and scientist in me were dubious.

Then, just two years later in 1974, as a 25-year-old psychotherapist fresh out of graduate school working in a rural hospital and mental health center in Xenia Ohio, a 22-year-old patient was referred to me by his surgeon. He had recently returned from a two-year tour in Vietnam as a foot soldier.

The young man's doctor wanted me to help him deal with the emotional aspects of having a full colostomy due to the colitis that ravaged his lower intestine and bowel. The surgery was scheduled for the following week. The young man was devastated to think that he would be wearing an excrement bag his entire adult life. I asked his doctor if the surgery could be delayed for six weeks so the patient could be better prepared. I could not bear to tell his doctor the truth that I wanted to treat his colitis with autogenics. My real fear was that practicing something as unproven as hypnosis and autogenics would result in failure and I would be laughed out of the hospital. The patient was willing to try anything, and practiced the exercises precisely.

Six weeks later, the young man showed no evidence of colitis and the surgery was cancelled. I was astounded and frightened by the results of my own treatment. The surgeon simply noted in the chart that the colitis had gone into remission and resolved on its own.

Then, in 1984, a nurse came to me to help with a difficult divorce from an abusive husband. About a year after the divorce she was back in my office suffering from a cancerous thyroid, most likely the result of radiation treatment she had received as a teenager for severe acne. She showed evidence of cancer in her lymph nodes and stomach cavity. The oncologists removed half of her thyroid, followed by chemotherapy and radiation treatment. The outlook was bleak and I didn't want to give her "false hope" for a positive outcome. We began what I started calling "targeted medical hypnosis training" along with traditional psychotherapy. She visualized her immune system as piranha fish devouring the cancerous cells. About three months later, she called one day to report that the piranha of her imagery had spontaneously changed to beautiful tropical saltwater fish and she knew she was recovering. Five years later, she was still free of cancer.

I have used targeted medical hypnosis in my psychotherapy practice for over 40 years with literally thousands of patients. A few were lost to either the ravages of their disease or iatrogenic (medical treatment) causes. The scientist in me is totally convinced it works, and the 11 year old is still in awe of its mystery.

———————

Since I wrote that article in 1981, it is my foray into Heart-Centered Hypnotherapy, Psychodrama in Trance and Breath Work starting in 1995 that proved to be my own life-changing discovery, and my modality of choice for effectively treating my clients along with my targeted medical hypnosis treatments.

It is so sad to me that "therapy" still has such negative stigma attached to it. Most people still hold the beloof that if you seek help from a therapist, you must be "crazy" or something in you is "broken" that must be "fixed." We carry so much shame when we experience difficulties in our lives. And yet it is these difficulties that provide the opportunity to become all that we can be. We all carry Karma and Existential Issues into our lives so that we can grow and improve and become enlightened. When we judge ourselves or others for entering into processes intended to heal our traumas and move us forward in our lives, we cut ourselves off from amazing opportunities available to us. Competent and effective therapy provides tools and experiences to heal ourselves and move forward. I am eternally grateful to the universe for providing me the opportunities I have described here, and pray that all might have the chance and the bravery to take similar paths.

# 26

# Water Babies

During the second year of our Internship Training and throughout our Personal Transformation Intensive Leadership training we can practice our breath work in hot tubs set at body temperature so as not to overheat. I jumped at the opportunity. I had taken and passed my scuba diving certification after moving to Seattle in the late 1970s and enjoyed diving in wetsuits in Puget Sound with Mary Anne's brother John.

On one dive in an underwater park they constructed next to the Edmonds Ferry Terminal using sunken boats to attract fish, we followed the guide rope down and were swimming along about 50 feet from the surface checking out the cold water sea life that lived on the bottom there. The visibility in Puget Sound is poor—perhaps fifteen feet on a good day in the very early spring before the algae is in bloom. But it was amazing to skim along the bottom poking at the small crabs ambling along, and disturbing the Petrale Sole so they would shake off their camouflage of bottom dirt and find a new spot to settle in. John had been in the Navy during the Vietnam War, so I always considered him to be more experienced and sensible in the water. That was my first mistake.

So I'm dutifully letting him take the lead, and we are having a great time swimming along the bottom and exploring when I hear a "bump, bump, bump" a bit to the left and overhead. Now you're really not supposed to hear much when you are

50 feet underwater, and if you do, it's probably not good news. So I cock my head up and around to take a look, and see the hint of two very large propellers swirling the water into millions of bubbles about 30 feet up in the murky water. It's the bubbles and the sound that are the giveaway.

The training to become certified as a scuba diver is rigorous, and thank God it is. I did not panic and John seemed oblivious, poking around the bottom to muster the crabs. I swam over to him and poked him in the side to get his attention. I wanted him to take note that we had swum directly under the ferry, and needed to get out of there pronto.

Now, if you point your index finger towards the surface, it means, "let's go up now," so I couldn't do that or he would think I was in trouble and wanted to surface. If you stick your thumb up, it means everything is OK, so that wouldn't help. So I made up my own signal: I pointed my index and middle finger at my eyes behind my mask like when Robert De Niro pointed at Ben Stiller in *Meet the Parents* to indicate he had his eyes on him, and then I pointed the same fingers straight up. Without a pause, John immediately looked up.

He looked back at me with saucer eyes, quickly checked his wrist compass, and took off like a shot for the beach, skimming along the bottom. I followed his fins all the way in. We didn't surface until we were in about four feet of water and could see the sun shining down on us from above.

So, going into three feet of water in a hot tub with a snorkel and nose plug seemed like a wonderful opportunity to relax. It would be quiet, and today I would have the tub to myself rather than being crowded in with the 30 other students in the main room on their mats noisily breathing and experiencing next to me.

Silly me…

So I enter the hot tub with my snorkel and nose plug carefully secured to my face. As soon as I put my face into the water, my body tenses up. The inside of my nose is on fire and I am sure my nose plug has slipped and I am breathing in water. I pull my head out of the water and sit up to adjust my nose plug. Certainly it's an equipment malfunction. I re-secure the nose plug and mask, and dip my face back in the water. I start to breathe through my snorkel, and again the sensation of toxic liquid being breathed into my nostrils is overpowering. Now I'm getting pissed off. Why can't David supply adequate equipment to do our breath work in the hot tub? However, I will not be denied. Then Diane's words come back to me again: "Trust your body…everything you are experiencing leads you back to the source."

"Fuck the source—I'm not getting anywhere here," my mind retorts.

"I'm not getting anywhere here," I hear myself say again.

Not getting anywhere…Not moving…Stuck…Entrapped…Toxic water…Shit—I'm back in my mother's womb again. I said I was done with this, dammit.

But it comes to me that there is something else I must resolve before I exit this drugged-out place for good.

Suddenly, I am aware of a rush of water and a loud whooshing sound over my right shoulder. I am immediately drawn to it. As I swim over to it, my cognitive mind interrupts and says, "That's the hot tub pump turning on," but my body is telling me different. The burning in my nose is gone. My third eye opens and my intuition speaks:

"That is the sound of the Source present in the water. Your Creator is with you here and was then." I recall my experiences during breath work; then is now and now is then.

Just as suddenly, I am aware of a sucking sound across the tub. I swim to it. My rational mind knows it is the hot tub water return that takes the water back to the pump to recirculate it back out again. Hmmm.

My body knows it is the memory of my mother's cervix opening so that I may begin my life breathing my own oxygen and finding my own path outside of her body that we have shared for the past nine months.

OK. Now what?

I swim back to the whooshing of the water flowing out of the pump. The water carries the voice of the creator to me.

"I am here. I will always be with you."

I swim back to the outflow port.

Oh my God! The chaos is palpable. I don't want any part of what's out there for me.

I swim back to the whooshing. "Your soul chose this as a part of your destiny. It is your choice. Don't be afraid. I am with you. I will always be with you."

"But my tribe out there believes you forgot them, abandoned them, sent them to certain destruction and death. They are pissed at you and don't want anything to do with you," I inform the source.

"I know," the whooshing whispers. "I can't do anything about that. The trauma of the Holocaust is too much for them to understand yet. They will need many lives to process what happened there. The family and the tribe you have chosen are deep in their beloofs. They must first deny God to return to God. It is part of how we survive trauma. With great suffering comes greater understanding, if one wishes."

"Family and tribe I have chosen?" I question.

"You asked to Teach Peace," I hear the Creator remind me.

"What?"

"You said you wanted to Teach Peace."

"Oh, that…" I remember.

I remember someone once told me, "Be careful what you ask for."

"This is your chance to teach your tribe how to find their way back to their Creator and find real peace."

I will be with you through it all," the whooshing reminds me.

———

I swim back over to the outlet port. I see light beaming through my closed eyes behind my snorkel mask. The light calls me out to my destiny. It is time for my birth, my beginning, this time. I am terrified, and then feel the touch of a strong hand on my shoulder. No one is in the tub with me. I quietly exit the tub alone under the tall Pine trees of our retreat center and remove my snorkel and nose plug. Light is beaming through the branches all around me. I am aware of the multitude of wildlife behind the trees accompanying me on my journey. I am acutely aware of being surrounded by the Mystery Beyond all Mysteries and experience deep peace under the warm sun. The spirits of the First Nation are gathered around me on this sacred ground we share. I feel the thousands of years that humans have lived on this land, grown their food, produced their offspring, suffered their traumas, fell down, lifted themselves up, murdered each other and loved each other, all in the natural cycle of life. I know that I am now a part of that cycle and that it is right. Everything is exactly as it is supposed to be.

It is what it is.

It was what it was.

It will be what it will be.
I am that I am.

———————

I dry myself off, take a quick shower, return to my cohort, and tell no one of my experience as it integrates into every cell of my being.

# 27

# Spirit Guide

To be a Spirit guide one must first be guided by Spirit. To be guided by Spirit, one must be connected to Spirit. To be connected to Spirit, one must be open to Spirit. To be open to Spirit, one must confront and resolve his beloofs.

That day in the water of the hot tub was one of those crystal clear moments in my life; I was transformed. When I first became a therapist, decades before I heard the word beloof slip from my mouth, when I took my first job as a caseworker with the Montgomery County Children's Services Board in Dayton Ohio at age 20, having just received my Bachelor's Degree in Psychology, I had no idea that Spirit had anything to do with life's equation. I was a scientist and an engineer in the spirit of my father and my oldest brother. I was applying the same principles to psychology, the study of human behavior.

My father, the architect and engineer, would say, "If you can't touch it, pick it up, turn it over, and put it back down, it doesn't exist." But then at the same time, he followed the laws of Kashrut in his daily practice, and recited all the prayers of Yom Kippur and Passover in traditional Hebrew. He taught religious school to the second graders in the Synagogue Sunday school and taught us to respect every religion on the planet. I overheard him say to our Catholic neighbors over the fence at Hanukkah and Christmas, "You keep praying up your pipe and I'll pray up mine—it's all going to the same place anyway." I didn't realize until after his death how deeply spiritual he was in his own uniquely quiet and non-judgmental way.

My brother Alan was a Chemical Engineer busy trying to find a way to pull the sludge out of Lake Erie and turn it into building bricks that didn't smell like human excrement. He never succeeded. He named himself an Atheist as a teenager and continued on that path his entire life. He passed at age 69 a devout Atheist.

My mother would say, "After you die you just lie in the cold, cold ground. I never heard her utter the word God unless it was followed by the word damn.

So when I won my National Institutes of Health grants in the mid-1990s, and was paid handsomely to show that hypnotic suggestions placed during recorded hypnosis sessions and then later triggered by electronic signals delivered to a patient in the form of a vibration device, it verified my beloof that science was the end point of knowledge: that when empirical evidence was found to either support or deny a hypothesis, then knowledge was achieved. Why else would NIH give me almost a million dollars in research monies?

And when I completed my research and statistically proved that hypnotic suggestions triggered by electronic signals worked significantly better than hypnosis without signals, I belooved that I had added to the body of "knowledge." However, I would come to understand much later that I had simply added to the body of "scientific" knowledge and not to the body of universal knowledge.

Through this work I have been doing, I have come to a deep understanding that "science" is a construct created by human beings and therefore based in human beloofs. I have come to believe that "science" is constructed much like religious institutions and that it has developed its own dogma. And I have come to see that the "medical" and "research" institutions that create and maintain the dogma of most of our health science is Allopathic Western Medicine and the Pharmaceutical Cartel. There is a large and growing contingent of health care providers like myself who share this understanding.

Bruce Lipton, a renowned and respected Doctor of Cell Biology and the author of *Biology of Beliefs* lectured to us at our National Wellness Conference in 2011. He told his personal story of presenting to the Dean of the University of Wisconsin School of Medicine where he taught and conducted cell research of his proven "scientific" findings that "disease" in the form of cell death is caused by changes in the environment of the cell rather than any anomaly internal to the cell. His research had furthered categorized the environmental changes that cause cell disease into three distinct types: (1) Trauma; (2) Toxins; and (3) Beliefs.

I immediately understood how trauma and toxins would cause injury to the cell. If I smacked my arm with a hammer, I would immediately feel intense pain, and the skin cells and tissues under my skin would turn black and blue. And if I poured sulfuric acid, a strong toxin over my skin, I would feel intense pain and it would burn and destroy my skin and the tissue under it.

But beliefs? Beliefs?

Bruce had "scientifically" proven that toxic beloofs traumatize our cells and contradict healing; that if a patient diagnosed with cancer maintained the beloof that they would die from the cancer, their physical cells would cooperate with that beloof and promptly kill the patient. And if that same patient directed healing beliefs toward their injured cells, they could heal. That's exactly how my young patient healed his colitis-ravaged colon and bowel so very many years before I learned of Lipton's findings.

The Dean responded by telling Bruce that he was "violating the dogma of medicine," and that his findings were "unacceptable." Bruce went on to tell us that he really didn't know the precise definition of "dogma" so he looked it up in Webster's dictionary. He paraphrased to us that dogma meant "religious beliefs without basis in science." So he finally understood: American medicine was a religion he must blindly follow or suffer excommunication.

Dr. Lipton left the Medical School at Wisconsin shortly after his conversation with the Dean, went to teach at the Saint George University Medical School in Granada, and continued his research independently. His work has been validated and replicated in many scientific venues, but has not been able to penetrate the venerated walls of Western Medicine.

My belief that it is crucial to introduce spiritual energy into the process of preventing and recovering from physical, emotional, and psychological suffering was proven to me that day in the hot tub, not in "scientific" research. I have come to a deep understanding as have most respected health care providers, that a strong Spiritual belief system is crucial to the prevention of, and recovery from, human disease. I can produce no "scientific," "empirical," "evidence based," "peer reviewed," or "recognized academic journal published" data to support my claims. My evidence was in the water that day.

I'm reminded of a song that Bonnie Raitt sings, called, "God Was In the Water that Day" written by Randall Bramblett and Davis Causey:

God was in the water that day
Pickin' through the roots and stones
Trippin' over sunken logs
Tryin' not to make his presence known
God was in the water that day
Wadin' in careful steps
Bubbles risin' from his feet
Comin' up from the muddy depths
Castin' out a line
Castin' out a line to the shadows
Castin' out a line but no one's biting
I am at my pitiful desk
Starin' at the colorless walls
Wishin' I was any place else
Down into a dream I fall
Sittin' in a tiny boat
Driftin' on the mindless sea
And if I disappear
At least I'm floating free
Castin' out a line
Castin' out a line to the darkness
Castin' out a line but no one's biting
God was in the air that day
Breathin' out a haunted breeze
Tryin' not to make a sound
Shufflin' through the dried up leaves
God was in the air that day
Circlin' like a drunken hawk
Sweepin' with a hungry eye
Over the ground I walk
Castin' out a line
Castin' out a line to the darkness

Castin' out a line but no one's biting
Castin' out a line
Castin' out a line to the shadows
Castin' out a line but no one's biting

Were the authors of the song channeling Carl Jung that day?

*"One does not become enlightened by imagining figures of light, but by making the darkness conscious."*
— C.G. Jung

If you had asked me back when I started working at Montgomery County Children's Services if I was on a path of spiritual healing, I would have recoiled from the idea. I would have responded, "I don't travel in the world of the occult. You'll have to ask your Rabbi or Priest or Minister about that; I am a psychotherapist. My job is to help you discover what has malfunctioned in your psyche." Back then, that was my dogma of psychology.

As I studied for my Master's Degree in Social Work at the University of Michigan Graduate School, my dogma changed. We learned about "systems theory" and "behaviorism." The dogma changed to looking at the relationship between people and social systems. That dogma made more sense to me on an intellectual level. However, it did nothing to ameliorate the anxiety and pain inside of me. It took me a few decades to discover that my journey was intended to heal myself, and that my injuries were primarily spiritual in nature.

Since 2003 I have been moving my life through the three distinct phases we teach in the PTI Three: Ego, Soul, Self. It is crystal clear to me that I am on a journey of discovery, spiritual healing, and ultimately transformation. As I become conscious of and connected to my spiritual being, my life falls into place. Starting with my introduction to my Higher Power through 12-Step recovery work in the mid-1990s, followed by the palpable connection with my Creator in the inter-life after the Revolutionary War, to my conversation with God in the water of the hot tub that day, I am continuing to relax into a relationship with mystery and unknowing. Dogma and dualism is replaced with discovery and paradox.

In the process, my mind slows and quiets allowing me to experience the moment I am in and no other. My knowing comes to me not through thinking, but in the process of being. That is how I write this manuscript at this very moment in time: without thought; from an empty mind; from the depth of my heart and soul so I might be ultimately authentic. I strive to be the same person no matter where I am or what I am doing. So the therapist is the father is the husband is the child is the grandchild is the grandfather.

I write these words from my heart and soul to the heart and soul of the collective. I write for my wife Mary Anne, my daughter Jessica, my daughter Liz, my brother Alan, my brother Michael, my father Jacob, my mother Sylvia. I write for my entire extended family and my ancestors in both directions; for those who came before, and for those who come after. I write for my Uncles who fought in Germany and came home with PTSD; for their wives and children who suffered with them, and for those anywhere and everywhere who have been touched by war and genocide. I write these words for those who died in the Holocaust, those who were spared, and for those who came after as I did. I write these words for the Nazis who participated in the Holocaust, for those who were spared, and for those who came after. I write these words to heal myself, and in some small way, heal the collective.

> May we see an end to the suffering of man's inhumanity
> to man.
> May we see the day when all humankind rises up to
> be our highest self.
> May we live in a world filled with love and joy!
> And may we all become Teachers of Peace.
> Aho!

# 28

# Preparing for This Ending

I've asked myself why I wish to write this memoir, and why now. At first I thought I wanted to leave my story in written form for my wife and children and close friends so they could have a recorded history of this person they have known for so many years from his own view. Then as I began to write, I realized I wanted to put my life to this point into a more conscious and connected form so I myself might understand the flow of my life better. Then, just a few months ago, I experienced a weekend retreat at our Wellness Mentor's program that forced my hand and started me writing. It was that damn breath work again, and it occurred in the hot tub.

Mentor's weekends are gatherings of the most advanced and experienced practitioners of our processes. We gather from all parts of the world to the retreat center in Issaquah Washington. For many it is truly a pilgrimage of thousands of miles from faraway places like South Africa, Israel, England, and all over the U.S. Mary Anne and I are blessed to be able to drive just 40 minutes to attend, although we also know it was part of our destiny to leave our birthplace of Dayton Ohio and plop in Seattle, not knowing consciously that we were being energetically drawn to the Mother Ship.

I don't share much about the processes we practice at Mentors except to say that they are sacred in nature and dip deeply into the symbology of Jungian thought and practice in an experiential way. Many years ago, one of our clients who traveled from Alaska to attend our PTI weekends was quizzed after each weekend by his curious wife. He brought us the perfect answer to the question of what we actually do at our weekends. He lovingly told his wife, "If you want to know, you've got to go." She did ultimately go, and understood that her personal experience of the processes defied any description her husband might give her. Each person's experience of the processes we teach is unique and personal. That is all I can say about our Mentor's weekends. However, it is possible for me to share my personal experience during the weekends rather than how the processes work.

During Mentor's weekends we practice advanced levels of experiential Jungian processes incorporating dream material and the symbology of the Tarot. It is our personal reactions to Tarot symbols, and to the symbols that appear in our dreams that can allow us to peer deeply into the hidden dark places of our psyche in a way that is not otherwise possible and bring them into our light. Here is how Carl Jung himself put it:

> There is a thinking in primordial images, in symbols which are older than the historical man, which are inborn in him from the earliest times, eternally living, outlasting all generations, still make up the groundwork of the human psyche. It is only possible to live the fullest life when we are in harmony with these symbols; wisdom is a return to them.

On this particular weekend, using the experience of the symbols that had come to me during sleep time, I was able to provide healing to the shadow parts of my Caretaker, my Tyrant, and my Trickster at the deepest level I had ever experienced.

Mary Anne and I work in the same Mentor's group at the same time with separate partners. We are working on our own personal issues, but doing so in the vibrational energy field of each other, the collective of our group, and the collective of humankind. Mary Anne and I don't know the specifics of what we are each working on, but are in each other's healing energy field. It has brought us a quality of relationship and closeness that is indescribable. Our souls are connected at a level of depth I never believed possible.

When people observe us, they see a normal married couple who have been living together for over 40 years. We bicker, snap, kiss, hug, get hurt, misunderstand, miscommunicate, dance, and work together. But if one could actually measure a soul connection, there is only a hair's-breath of space between her soul and mine, if at all. So when we do our Mentor's work on the same weekend at the same time, our energy fields are intertwined in a sacred dance of healing and recovery and connection. We don't talk to each other much during those weekends, and yet our cells are talking with each other continuously. It has allowed us to practice together and teach together in our PTI Groups at a depth of connection rarely found.

My mentor's work that weekend occurred at such unconscious depth that I cannot for the life of me remember what happened in the work that led me to my breath work session in the hot tub on Sunday. It really doesn't matter if I remember on a conscious level or not. I suppose I could go back and review my notes of the weekend. If I were at the University of Michigan Graduate School, or working as I had as a Principal Investigator for the National Institutes of Health, I would have taken a test or written a detailed report of my findings. And in that process of trying to move my experience from the cellular to the cognitive, I could lose its healing properties. So usually, I just rest and meditate after our weekends.

But back to that damn hot tub and that damn breath work.

So there I am, ready for a relaxing and integrative breath work session, and this time, I actually got one! But what I experienced was mind blowing.

The day is beautiful: warm and sunny with light filtering through the tall pines of the foothills of the Cascade Mountains. I begin breathing through my snorkel and lower my head into the water. Breathing under water always gets me connected to my breath and to my body. It was the same when I would scuba dive. The sound of my own breath entering and leaving my lungs is amplified by the surrounding water. With each breath I begin slipping deeper and deeper into that now familiar twilight of trance. Trance is merely a sublimely relaxed state that allows me a slightly altered state of consciousness. It may be just a single degree of variance. They say if an asteroid is on a collision course with the earth, if we alter its course just a single degree, the asteroid harmlessly passes by. So it is with trance.

So with each breath I hear drawing through the plastic tube of my snorkel, my consciousness alters a single degree. My biased observer begins to stand down and my beloofs start to release their hold on my experience. My body is floating physically and psychically. I am conscious of the merger of my creator and myself; a sensation of my body and soul being held and rocked in loving arms. When my beloofs of doubt and uncertainty sneak into the water, I make a choice of courage. *"God, grant me the serenity to accept the things I cannot change, the courage to change the things I can, and the wisdom to know the difference."* I allow paradox to prevail;

186 | Of Endings and Beginnings

that my experience is both real and unreal, correct and incorrect at the same time. Paradox ends the debate, and I simply relax and engage in my experience.

So here I float, both in my body and outside my body at the same time. I begin to encounter a container around me. And then the presence of another being, a person that surrounds me. "Shit. I'm back in the womb," I think.

I thought I was done here, but something is different. I'm not drugged, and neither is she. I begin exploring the sensation of this womb. It is different from before. I can feel it. "I" am contained in another body. And the container around me; she is not my mother of this life. And the body I reside in this time, it's not the body of this life I am experiencing floating in the hot tub of Wellness.

I immediately become crystal clear; it is undeniable. I have entered the experience of another beginning; clearly, my next beginning. My cognitive presence is about to explode.

I experience a moment of panic. Am I dying in this life and about to begin another? What about Mary Anne? What about Jessica? What about Liz?

Breathe...Breathe...Breathe...

I am downloading information from the collective. It is really quite simple.

This is my future. There will be another beginning after the next ending, and again after that, and again after that. That's all the information available to me now, and frankly, I wish to have no more. Enough mind blowing for today. I consciously pull my consciousness out of that womb and return it to the warm water of the hot tub.

It is also crystal clear that I am not yet finished with this life. There is so much more to learn, so much more living with Mary Anne and Jessica and Liz. I know I have more to experience, to learn, and to teach.

Possible? Illusion? Delusion? You can decide—if that's important to you.

Ultimately, experiencing my next womb and my next body makes it crystal clear why I have chosen to write this memoir now: I am entering the final chapters of this life and must prepare for my ending this time. Perhaps it will be many years from now, or perhaps just a few. *"God, grant me the serenity to accept the things I cannot change..."* I try to keep my body and spirit as healthy as possible, and I actively envision four score and ten, but then again, shit happens.

When I was small and unaware of my spiritual injuries and disconnection, death terrified me. Death was the image of the bodies piled on top of each other, emaciated, terrified eyes staring out of lifeless bodies in horror. And then there was the beloof of my mother who said, "After you die you just lie there in the cold, cold ground." Really, Mom? And then my spiritual but quiet father who never spoke to me about death, but seemed to have a peace within about dying. I used to try to comfort myself with a dualistic metaphor: "I was OK before I came into this life, so I'm sure I'll be OK after I leave it." It helped, but not much.

With all my work, and that amazing breath work in the hot tub that day, all is possible and nothing is possible. Fear is a beloof. Belief is an option. I release my fear and submit to the divine.

# 29

# Epilogue

Back home a few days after my mind-blowing experience in the hot tub at Wellness, I awake at 3:00 AM. I am in that place of wakeful dreaming. Without thought, I walk from my bed to my computer to write. Within minutes I finish my writing, return to my bed to lie back down next to Mary Anne, and fall into a deep and restful sleep. Here is what I wrote:

I am called in the darkness of the mid-night
Called away from my sleep
My mind awakens against my will
I am awake but wish to sleep
"Not tonight," a voice within whispers

I understand in a way you can only begin to imagine
We function in a way unknown to ourselves
Listen for the voice that no one hears
That speaks in a foreign tongue
Listen for the messages from the cosmos
Listen in a way we never learned
But we have always known
It comes to us in our sleep
Often unheard lest we listen with other ears
It calls to us as we sleep

When we listen closely we awaken within
Awaken to the still small voice from the cosmos
Calling to us about our destiny

Calling us to wake up and listen with our conscious mind
Lest we miss the call
Calling us to action
Calling us to believe
Calling us to submit
So I awaken to listen

The language is unknown to me
But known to me at the deepest level I imagine
I listen with ears unknown to me
Yet always known to me
I listen with my cells

It is awakening calling me
"Wake up and listen," it says without language
"Then speak in a way I understand," I demand
"Not how I work," I hear
So I listen with different ears

My cells listen and accept
A knowing that comes from the ethos
Not from within
Not from my mind
My mind sleeps in the darkness
My soul hears every word
Calling me to action
Calling me to believe
Calling me to submit
So I awaken to listen

I have come to love living in the world of paradox. I play in the playground of the quantum in a way I was never able to play as a child. I continue to move further into healing the

Karmic and existential fear I brought with me into this life and acquired during this life, and allow my soul and authentic self to emerge from a healing ego. I live comfortably in a world where nothing is true and everything is true. I accept that I know nothing, and that I know everything.

My daughter Liz taught me to abandon the world of "diagnoses." She showed me that all "mental health" diagnoses are based in beloofs. As I watched her struggle, trying to discern "reality" from "delusion," I had to ask myself, "Do I really have the audacity to believe that my experience is 'reality' and hers is 'delusion'? And the medications they give her to bring her back from 'delusion' to 'reality'; there is as much potential that such medication forced her from her 'reality' to *our* 'delusion'.

During graduate school at the University of Michigan we studied the work of R. D. Laing, M.D. Along with others of his day, Laing was considered part of the "anti-psychiatry" movement. Although Laing recognized that people experienced severe emotional distress, he rejected the notion that mental illness was a strictly biological event without taking into account, social, emotional, intellectual, and psychological issues.

In 1965 R. D. Laing and his colleagues used a deserted nursery school known as Kingsley Hall to create a community for themselves and people in a state of psychosis. As a result, Kingsley Hall became home to the Philadelphia Association and one of the most radical experiments in psychiatry. Laing considered that psychosis is a state of reality like living in a waking dream, and not an illness to be eliminated. In some cultures, delusions are considered a state of trance valued as mystical or Shamanistic. Laing's experiments sought to allow schizophrenic people a space to explore their delusions and internal chaos. Residents were treated with kindness and respect and staff used interpersonal interaction to help bring patients into a place of safety.

One notable resident of the Philadelphia Association was Mary Barnes. Along with resident psychiatrist Joseph Berke, Mary later went on to write *Two Accounts of a Journey Through Madness*, describing her stay at Kingsley Hall and use of her mental condition as a vehicle for painting and creative expression. Her account became famous in the 1970s when it was used as the basis for the play, "Mary Barnes," by David Edgar. (Condensed from Wikipedia.)

In his book T*he Politics of Experience*, Laing said, "If the human race survives, future men will, I suspect, look back on our enlightened epoch as a veritable age of Darkness. They will presumably be able to savor the irony of the situation with more amusement than we can extract from it. The laugh's on us. They will see that what we call 'schizophrenia' was one of the forms in which, often through quite ordinary people, the light began to break through the cracks in our all-too-closed minds."

Inspired by the work of American psychotherapist Elizabeth Fehr, Laing began to develop a team offering "rebirthing workshops" in which one designated person chooses to re-experience the struggle of trying to break out of the birth canal represented by the remaining members of the group who surround him or her. Interestingly, David and Diane, in creating Heart-Centered Hypnotherapy may have channeled some of their theory from the work of Laing. As I've described my own travels back to the womb, rebirthing is a major part of our practice.

Not much of Laing's work in the 1960s and 1970s made its way into the modern practice of psychiatry. My daughter Liz suffered mightily through her unfortunate visits to the emergency room and the psych unit. My heart still hurts remembering how I looked on powerlessly as she was "treated" psychiatrically. Blasted with medication and ignored as if she didn't exist, she would sit on her bed alone in silence during her brief stays, or go out on smoke breaks with the other residents. There was a modicum of "kindness and respect" there, but not much.

Liz's recovery since that time has been remarkable in spite of the traditional psychiatry she was exposed to. Most times she came out more confused about her experience rather than clearer. Liz ultimately completed her Bachelor's Degree in Sociology with high honors and won a prestigious award as first in her class. Currently she works as a case manager for a social service agency serving high-risk youth. She lives independently and has literally hundreds of loving friends.

I don't know if Liz will ever believe what an amazing teacher she has been for me. She still struggles with the beloofs she acquired during her episodes in "treatment," that she is somehow "broken," that her biochemical makeup is "defective," and that she will struggle with her "condition" throughout her life. I have wished at times that I could simply reach into her beloof system and gently press the "off" button. But it's not for me to do. I feel guilt for the times I tried to bully her into my way of processing her experience. I know it's none of my business. This is her life, her Karma, her beginning, not mine. When I simply love her completely, Liz and I do just fine just like Jessica and I, and Mary Anne and I, and everyone and I.

In the process of being "insane," Liz proved to me that sanity and insanity co-exist in the same moment. She taught me that delusion is reality and reality is delusion. That Schrödinger's cat is both alive and dead at the same moment, depending on the people and process that observes or does not observe the cat's condition.

The mental health professional inside of me has come to believe that in today's standard of mental health treatment, the cartels of medicine and psychopharmacology have prevailed: their beloofs reside deep inside of most of us; that handing out drugs to manage mental, emotional, psychological, and spiritual trauma is cheap and easy. In the process, drugs companies make huge profits and insurance companies save billions of dollars. And millions of individuals become addicted to all sorts of licit and illicit drugs without healing the underlying source of their suffering. I'm sorry, but sometimes I just have to rant.

My heart cries out for Liz's complete healing. My heart cries out for the healing of all who suffer from affliction and their search for peace. My heart cries out for the "mentally ill," the "addicted," the "lonely," the "depressed," the "panic stricken:" all those who suffer from "illness" and "dis-ease."

May we all practice compassion and understanding towards ourselves and each other as we discover that pain in inevitable and "suffering" is optional.

May we each discover the universal peace that is available to us all.

---

I have come to deeply understand that for the simple and humble human being that is me, in my world of the paradox, in my universe of the quantum, all observations and judgments are right and wrong concurrently. My world is a universe of infinite potentiality. Two plus two can equal three, or four, or five. Now might be the past, or the future, or all three simultaneously. Time stands still, regresses backwards, and progresses forward all at the same time until I decide how I wish to observe time. Did my presence in my mother's womb in this life represent travel back in time, and my presence in a new womb represent travel forward in time—or both, or neither? If I wish, I can simply giggle, play with it all, experience my feelings, and move on to my next experience.

I relinquish all responsibility for any outcome other than what I can influence directly: *"the courage to change the things I can."* All else resides within the responsibility of the universe and the divine—certainly somewhere above my pay grade. All beings become my cohort: my family members, my friends, my clients, and the people I come in contact with at the Safeway store; everything with living cells—the plants and the animals. All beings have the potential to be one I can love, and one who can love me.

Entering the world of the paradox, the universe of the quantum, requires me to become completely conscious of my unconscious beloofs. My beloofs were born into, and reside within the darkness of my trauma. When I recover the origins of my beloofs and raise them to conscious awareness, heal the trauma that birthed them, and in the process see how they dis-serve me, I can release them into the light and open myself to the limitless potential of the universe.

May I be open to receive the limitless potential of the universe.

May I be open to receive the limitless potential of the universe.

May I be open to receive the limitless potential of
the universe.
May I always teach peace.
And may we all teach peace.
I love you…

CPSIA information can be obtained
at www.ICGtesting.com
Printed in the USA
FSOW02n0733230116
15881FS

9 780937 977064